CW01456507

BREATHING TECHNIQUES: A GUIDE TO MINDFULNESS

The Complete Guide To Improve Self Healing, Self Control, Concentration, Happiness And To Reduce Anxiety

SAMUEL FINCH

© **Copyright 2020 by Samuel Finch**
All rights reserved.

This document is geared towards providing exact and reliable information with regards to the topic and issue covered. The publication is sold with the idea that the publisher is not required to render accounting, officially permitted, or otherwise, qualified services. If advice is necessary, legal or professional, a practiced individual in the profession should be ordered.

- From a Declaration of Principles which was accepted and approved equally by a Committee of the American Bar Association and a Committee of Publishers and Associations.

In no way is it legal to reproduce, duplicate, or transmit any part of this document in either electronic means or in printed format. Recording of this publication is strictly prohibited and any storage of this document is not allowed unless with written permission from the publisher. All rights reserved.

The information provided herein is stated to be truthful and consistent, in that any liability, in terms of inattention or otherwise, by any usage or abuse of any policies, processes, or directions contained within is the solitary and utter responsibility of the recipient reader. Under no circumstances will any legal responsibility or blame be held against the publisher for any reparation, damages, or monetary loss due to the information herein, either directly or indirectly.

Respective authors own all copyrights not held by the publisher.

The information herein is offered for informational purposes solely, and is universal as so. The presentation of the information is without contract or any type of guarantee assurance.

The trademarks that are used are without any consent, and the publication of the trademark is without permission or backing by the trademark owner. All trademarks and brands within this book are for clarifying purposes only and are the owned by the owners themselves, not affiliated with this document.

TABLE OF CONTENTS

INTRODUCTION

The breath is the result of action and breathing; It is a process by which living things absorb and expel air, taking part in the substances that compose it. Also, the concept of respiration is referred to the process by which cells release stored energy from food; through oxidation where nutrients combine with oxygen in the air to release useful energy, and carbon dioxide and water vapor are also produced as by-products, this is known as "cellular respiration."

To know what respiration is, it refers to an authentic biological process of every living being, and whose primary purpose is to sustain the activity of your organism (that is, alive) by exchanging carbon dioxide for oxygen.

The definition of respiration commonly refers to that it is a mechanism by which living beings inhale air, but it is only a demonstration of the respiratory system whose development mechanism is much more complicated, where the cells of organisms are benefited, in the so-called internal breathing.

The concept of internal or cellular respiration is different. Since the meaning of cellular respiration refers to a group of biochemical reactions by which certain organic compounds are destroyed in the inner part of the cell, due to oxidation. This metabolic system requires oxygen since it supplies the energy recycled by the cell (mainly in the form of ATP).

For aerobic living organisms, respiration represents a fundamental physiological method for life. It refers to a process of gas exchange with the environment that can be put into operation in different ways (by branchial, pulmonary, cutaneous, etc.).

Humans perceive oxygen through inspiration and then exhale carbon dioxide. At the moment of birth, when the baby is separated from the umbilical cord, breathing is the first independent act of the newborn. It is important to note that while an individual can tolerate several days without drinking or eating, they cannot go more than a few minutes without breathing. In this book, you will learn to Improve Self-Healing, Self-Control, Concentration, Happiness, and to Reduce Anxiety.

CHAPTER 1

THE HEALTH BENEFIT OF BREATHING

It is an almost automatic process that guarantees the oxygen supply, but... do we breathe correctly? Learning a good breathing routine will help us improve our health.

Did you know that deep breathing can help us eliminate toxins more effectively and even fight pain thanks to the release of endorphins?

Deep breathing or slow breathing gives calm and well-being to the person who practices it regularly.

This type of technique, where the person gets used to taking deep breaths, retaining that oxygen and exhaling it at the same time, is prevalent in yoga or mindfulness.

However, it should be said that, beyond these practices that have that classic link with Buddhism and meditation, they are not very common in our day to day.

Thus, very few times do we even stop to think "how we breathe."

Now, as an interesting fact, it is important to know that scientists from Stanford University have prepared an interesting study that shows how this type of breathing can benefit us.

Mark Krasnow, the biochemist, and director of this work, even explains that a small group of neurons has been identified that mediate between this type of respiration and relaxation, attention, and even efficacy to regulate emotions and reduce anxiety.

We are, without a doubt, facing a simple and accessible strategy that we should all practice. Just open your mouth and breathe deeply, calmly, and slowly.

1. Deep breathing to regulate stress and anxiety

According to this study by the University of Pisa (Italy), breathing can help calm and regulate anxiety attacks.

Breathing is an action that we carry out involuntarily. We inhale oxygen to obtain and create energy at the cellular level.

Then we exhale carbon dioxide, that by-product of cellular respiration.

This almost magical process benefits us remarkably as long as it is carried out in a slow, rhythmic, and profound way:

- However, something that most have experienced at some time is that, when we are scared or when we feel panic, our breathing becomes ragged and very fast: this process above breaks and is altered, causing the heart to "shoot."
- Meanwhile, deep breathing is capable of regular the parasympathetic nervous system to stimulate a relaxed state: the heart enters calm and mind.

By supplying our body with oxygen in a more leisurely, constant, and regular way, our muscles also stop being tense.

It is then when the sympathetic system, for its part, stops sending its high peaks of cortisol and adrenaline to our body.

Our whole body and mind enter a very suitable state of calm.

2. We eliminate toxins

This is interesting: our bodies are designed to release much of its toxins through respiration:

- Carbon dioxide is a natural toxic residue that comes from the metabolic processes of our body and, therefore, must be expelled regularly.
- However, when our lungs are used to taking rapid breaths, we do not fully expel these waste elements.

It would be very convenient for us to become aware of this, and that, at least for 2 or 3 times a day, we spend at least 10 minutes breathing deeply.

3. We decrease the sensation of pain

Something we often do almost unconsciously when we feel pain is holding our breath.

It is a natural mechanism of our brain when we receive a blow, an impact when we are injured.

However, and in the case of chronic and regular pain due to arthritis, lupus, or fibromyalgia, we will do very well.

Try holding your breath for a few seconds and breathing deeply and slowly.

In this way, we will release endorphins, those body's natural pain relievers. Similarly, this study by the University of Regensburg (Germany) emphasizes the soothing effect of good breathing.

4. It will help us improve our posture

Something as easy as practicing deep breathing from today will allow us to improve our body scheme and, above all, the back-neck axis.

By filling our lungs with the air, we can stimulate the spine to place it in a more harmonious, balanced, and correct posture.

Do not hesitate to try it.

5. We stimulate the lymphatic system

The lymphatic system is an essential part of the body's immune system and is made up of a complex network of lymphatic vessels, tissues, organs, and lymph nodes that fulfill many functions.

One of them, the one carried out by the lymphatic fluid, is to release from our body the remains of dead cells and other waste.

Deep breathing will help us achieve this, according to this research by Flinders University (Australia).

6. Take care of our hearts

Something interesting to know is also that aerobic exercise (cardio) uses fat for energy, while anaerobic exercise (strength training) uses glucose for energy.

However, if we get used to practicing the deep breathing "exercise" every day, we will be doing a fabulous cardio routine. This is stated in this study by the Govt Medical College (India).

7. We improve digestion

Deep breathing improves our digestion. Guess in what way?:

- We provide our body with more oxygen, and on a more regular basis, we also supply it to the digestive organs so that they work more efficiently.
- Besides, we increase blood flow and, in turn, stimulate intestinal action.
- It regulates the nervous system. Thus we feel calmer, and digestion is carried out calmly and efficiently.

CHAPTER 2

WHY THE CORRECT BREATHING TECHNIQUE HAS A GREAT INFLUENCE ON OUR BODY

Not breathing properly can cause chronic fatigue, digestive diseases, increased risk of cardiovascular accidents, or accumulated tension in the neck and shoulders.

The breath is a biological function of living beings by which oxygen is absorbed, dissolved in air or water, and carbon dioxide is expelled. The vast majority of people unconsciously carry out this action, which is necessary to maintain vital functions (all cells in the body need oxygen to function), and we rarely stop to think about whether we do it correctly or not. However, breathing is much more than filling the lungs with air. Its function is not only physiological; good oxygenation is synonymous with both physical and mental health and the key to well-being.

Not performing this 'mechanical' action correctly can cause chronic fatigue, digestive diseases, increased risk of cardiovascular accidents, accumulated tension in the neck and shoulders, or lack of concentration and memory loss. Fortunately, we can learn to breathe again and do it correctly to avoid these negative consequences in the medium and long term, in addition to enjoying a good level of energy and correct supply of oxygen.

Conscious breathing and emotions

By breathing correctly, we gain vitality. Improving breathing benefits the heart and cells, and therefore we get more energy. Furthermore, according to research carried out by the University of Toho School of Medicine (Japan), taking a deep breath contributes to a calm state, so that breathing is narrowing linked to our emotions. In this sense, the concept of 'conscious breathing' comes into play, the key piece for mind and body control. It is a way to focus total attention on the process of inhaling and exhaling air.

The technique is, a priori, simple and consists of slowing down the breathing movements and beginning to fill the lungs towards their deepest area. This is known as 'diaphragmatic breathing.' If you are a beginner, place one hand on your chest, at the level of the lungs, and another on your abdomen. Next, inhale feeling the air puff up your belly instead of just reaching your upper chest. The hands will indicate progress.

Benefits of correct oxygenation

- **Emotional control:** We have to breathe thinking about that action that we are doing, controlling the rhythm and depth. This helps the mind to focus on the body itself and forget negative thoughts. You will see how stress and anxiety are significantly reduced
- **Concentration:** By focusing on the breath, our minds will be training so that we can give our full attention to one action at a time whenever necessary
- **Muscle relaxation:** By slowing down breathing movements, filling the lungs slows down your heart rate, thereby de-stressing your muscles.
- **Elimination of toxins:** By improving our oxygenation, the oxygen that reaches our organs is exchanged for toxic substances that we do not need. Besides, it improves circulation and promotes regular digestion.

How To Use Breathing To Regain Your Inner Balance

If you want to eliminate the feeling of stress from your body and enjoy relaxation, concentration, and calm, you have to learn this simple breathing technique.

He breathes awareness is a powerful tool that provides support for yoga and meditation, producing or series of sensations in our body that help us to experience positive changes to both physical and psychological levels.

Square breathing is one of the main types of breathing that helps balance the body and mind and relax anxiety states. Its origin is found in the training of the US Navy SEALS, which uses it to maintain concentration and calm when faced with stressful situations.

How to make the square breath

Before you start breathing, you can sit with your back upright, in a meditation (or pranayama) posture. Once you feel comfortable, close your eyes and breathe freely, without worrying too much about the technique and without forcing yourself.

Square breathing is done in four times of 4 seconds each and is always done through the nose:

Step 1: Take a deep breath in through your nose for 4 seconds. Then hold the air for another 4 seconds more. The moment of inspiration is associated with happiness and recharging ourselves with energy. The retention of breath in the lungs represents the expansion of life throughout our bodies.

Step 2: It is the moment of exhalation, which must last another 4 seconds in which we empty the lungs. Now hold the exhale for another 4 seconds more. The expiration is associated with abandonment, darkness, and sadness, but it also helps us to remove everything negative and leave the lungs ready to oxygenate themselves. Holding your breath when your lungs are empty represents loneliness and symbolic death.

All parts of the breath must last the same. When you finish both inspiring and expiring, it is important that you feel comfortable. If you see that any of the phases cost you too much, reduce the time of all of them. If they are not all the same, they no longer form a square, and the symbol of the balance must form, with its four sides and four identical angles. As you gain practice, you can add a second if you want.

CHAPTER 3

BREATHING TECHNIQUES TO COMBAT STRESS

Did you know that there are certain ways of breathing that could contribute to stress reduction? At first, it may be somewhat complicated to put into practice the four techniques that we teach you in this chapter. But, over time, you will not only get it, but you will feel less tense.

Surely, you will have experienced a situation of stress or anxiety on more than one occasion. And very probably you have also noticed that, in those situations, you breathe in a fast and uncomfortable way. And it is not for less.

Stress and anxiety are coping mechanisms. They are intended to help us evade a situation that the brain interprets as harmful or dangerous. It should also be remembered that the response of the sympathetic nervous system to these feelings is very intense.

Not for pleasure, in these situations, the heart accelerates, the pulsations increase, and we breathe irregularly. It seems logical then that the risk of suffering, among many other conditions, heart attacks, angina and strokes, increases.

But have you ever wondered why? It should be remembered that bad breath results in our organs, not getting the oxygen they need to function properly. This situation of stress for the organism almost always leaves sequels, especially when such situations persist for a long period.

At this point, it is imperative to stop to analyze what is happening to us to look for possible solutions. The need to better manage emotions will then prevail. Breathing correctly could be another very useful resource for reducing stress. So here are four techniques that could help you reach the goal of learning to breathe better.

1. The square breath

Square breathing is the simplest of all breathing techniques. It is also known as samavriti pranayama. You could do it in bed, 20 minutes before sleeping. It will help you relax and rest deeply.

Steps:

- Sit on the bed with your back straight and your legs crossed.
- Breathe deeply for 3 minutes, trying to relax.
- Now, breathe in for 3 seconds, hold the air for another 3 seconds. And finally, breathe out for another 3 seconds.
- After a short rest, repeat the same steps, increasing the duration of such intervals to 4 seconds.

As you make this routine of breathing exercises a habit, you can increase the time between each step until you reach 7 seconds or 8 seconds.

2. Abdominal breathing

With square breathing, what you do is inflate your chest. The goal of abdominal breathing is now to focus on breathing on the diaphragm. This is a very effective technique to treat stress, contained tension, and anxiety.

Steps:

- Lie down on the bed or a quilt comfortably.
- Place one hand on your chest and one on your belly.
- Take a deep breath in through your nose for about 3 seconds. You will notice how your belly swells while the upper chest is stretched.
- Then exhale little by little for about 4 seconds.

Ideally, this routine should be performed ten times. Try to do them very slowly. Imagine how the diaphragm will help you focus on this breathing exercise.

3. Alternate nasal breathing

Alternative nasal breathing may seem strange to us if we have never practiced it. Therefore, the idea is to practice a little every day. You will gradually notice its benefits. When you get used to it, you will notice not only that it will help you channel and release stress. Also, to direct your attention only to what you are doing.

Steps:

- Sit so that you feel comfortable. However, make sure that your back is straight.
- Relax for a few minutes.
- Bring your right thumb up to your nose to cover the right nostril.
- Take a deep breath through the left nostril.
- When you feel your lungs have filled to the point where you cannot breathe more air, close the left nostril with your right ring finger.
- Exhale through the right nostril.
- Do the same thing again, but in reverse. That is, once you have taken as much air as possible with the right nostril, close it and exhale through the left nostril.

It may seem a little complicated at first. In all likelihood, you will need to be aware of covering one pit and opening the other. However, as you repeat it, the exercise will become more rhythmic and relaxing.

4. Consistent breathing

Consistent breathing also requires practice and patience. We invite you always to try it, adapting it to your abilities and personal characteristics. When you have managed to control it, you will feel more comfortable with yourself, and your whole body will thank you.

Consistent breathing consists of breathing five times per minute. In this way, the heart rate is optimized, and you will be able to relax the nervous system. It is an effective way to channel accumulated tension in situations of stress and anxiety. Practicing it will be of great help.

Steps:

- Sit with your back straight.
- Put a clock in front of you.
- The goal is to inspire and expire five times for a single minute. However, it is recommended that you first test your ability to control breathing. If you found that you couldn't distribute them over 1 minute, start by doing 6 or 7 inspirations and expirations.
- However, when you manage to distribute them in just 1 minute, you will see that you feel much better.

Breathing in Yoga

Fire breathing is a beneficial breathing technique for the body, but it must be done with caution, and if we are not used to it, under the supervision of an instructor.

Pranayama is the breathing technique in yoga and is made up of various breathing exercises that complement the asanas of each yogic modality. Fire breathing is one of those pranayamas and has multiple benefits for the body.

One of the most important factors within yoga is breathing because it allows the yogi to relax by inhaling and exhaling deeply while performing the asanas. Calm the mind, release tension, and oxygenate the brain.

What is fire breathing?

The Sanskrit name for fire breathing is "kapalabhati," where "kapala" is translated as "skull" and "bhati" as "cleanse." This refers to the cleansing of the mind.

Exercise helps control anxiety, nerves, worry, sadness, pain, fear, etc. The most common posture to do this pranayama is that of the lotus.

How is it done?

It consists of inhaling softly (if you are a beginner) and deeply through the nose to fill the lungs, and exhaling vigorously to expel all the air.

Expiration is also done with the nose, and the abdomen must be contracted towards the spine, this stimulates the diaphragm.

The rhythm of the breaths increases as the student masters the technique.

What are its benefits?

Practicing fire breathing has multiple benefits, mostly related to the emotionality and the functioning of the organism.

1. Regain control over stressful situations

Breathing in a controlled way increases concentration and cleanses the mind of negative energies, including stress. When we are stressed, the diaphragm contracts inward, just towards the area of the solar plexus, which is where all our emotions are stored.

With fire breathing, emotions can flow and leave our body, if necessary, to balance our body and improve mental and physical health.

2. Purifies blood and expels toxins from the lungs

It improves circulation, and the blood is purified due to the amount of oxygen it receives. Deep and complete inhalations and exhalations also purify the respiratory channel.

By expelling all the air, there is no residue of it inside the system, and new and cleaner air reaches the lungs when it is inhaled again.

3. Increase lung capacity

Humans do not typically use their lungs to their fullest capacity because they breathe in limited ways. They take short breaths that do not fill the lungs with air.

If fire breathing is practiced frequently, the lungs will become accustomed to gradually storing more air.

4. Strengthens the navel chakra, which is the third

This chakra, also called Manipura, is in charge of concentrating the emotions. It is the largest and most powerful chakra of all. It is related to our actions and emotions.

Have you ever felt an "empty stomach" when you are scared or sad? It is probably due to the manifestation of the chakra in our bodies.

5. It helps memory and concentration

By taking deep breaths, not only does the blood become oxygenated, the brain does too.

This increases our cognitive abilities and concentration because the brain works properly.

6. Stimulates the functioning of the digestive system

The digestive system is activated due to the constant movement of the diaphragm while performing the breathing exercise.

In this way, we also obtain improvements in digestion and prevent stomach upset.

Cautions

- If you are starting to practice fire breathing, always do it under the supervision of your instructor until you learn to master it. It is a delicate technique that needs time and patience.

- Don't take fire breaths so fast if you are a beginner because you can get dizzy. Your respiratory system is not used to quickly receiving and expelling so much air. Let him gradually get used to it, so you don't overload him.
- If you get dizzy, stop exercising. Do not continue if you start to feel bad because, because of the sudden shock of the air inside your lungs, they will tire and could make you pass out.
- Listen to your body, and the important thing is always to maintain a healthy workout.

Contraindications

This exercise is contraindicated for pregnant or menstruating women. It is also not recommended for patients who have epilepsy, hypertension, pulmonary emphysema, or cardiovascular diseases.

Fire breathing is undoubtedly a beneficial technique for your health because it increases your mental and lung capacity. You will be able to concentrate on everything that happens inside you, and it will make you more aware of your being.

However, it is an exercise that should be done with caution if you are just a beginner or even if you have already done it before, but you want to demand a little more from your body. The key to yoga is to be patient. You will not see the progress from one day to the next, but surely you will perceive it at some point.

CHAPTER 4

EMOTIONAL BENEFITS OF BREATHING EXERCISES

Breathing exercises can be of great help in combating anxiety problems and can even favor a better concentration if we are saturated.

Emotions, thoughts and the bodywork is a single nucleus. Whatever happens in one of them manifests in the other. You could say that it is almost impossible for everyone to act on their own. In this sense, it is very important to take into account certain breathing exercises to control the whole.

Likewise, and for this reason, when we find ourselves in some situation in our life, we must take into account how each one of the acts and the repercussion that what has happened in the others has.

Breathing has a great impact on physical and mental health. Also, it reflects emotions, moods, our relationship with the environment, feelings, and the state of our body. Therefore, we must learn some breathing exercises to manage emotions successfully.

Breathing Exercises

1. Renewal

Breathing fresh air helps us renew ourselves inside. It fills us with inner peace, cleanses negative energies, fills us with serenity, and calms worries.

Therefore, it is recommended, after a day or a week of hard work, to retire to a cool place away from the city and pollution, and take breathing sessions. Thus we will connect with the aroma and sound of nature.

2. Find solutions

Doing breathing therapies in places that please us generates a feeling of well-being and freedom.

So, taking a walk somewhere we like, while taking a deep breath, can lead us to the solution to a problem we had during the day. In this way, we will be thinking about your solution without the weight of stress and anxiety.

3. Improve concentration

When we do breathing therapy, we allow ourselves to get to know ourselves inwardly in a deeper way, coming out of reality, and changing negative thoughts to positive ones.

In this way, we begin to see things with a better disposition, and we encourage ourselves to move forward without fear or hindrance.

4. It transports us to wonderful places

With these breathing exercises, if we apply a good concentration, we can reach unimaginable places. We will set the imagination flying, thus managing to channel those energies that generate so much weight and leave them in that space.

In the end, we will return regenerated and with a clean aura.

5. It fills us with calm

If we take a few minutes to take a deep breath amid stress, anger, or rage, we will reach a state of calm with ourselves and the environment.

Just take ten deep breaths before acting or saying something or making an important decision.

6. Purify the spirit and remove mental blocks

Breathing helps us purify our lungs and our body. Also, it helps us control the stress levels caused by day-to-day setbacks.

At times when we feel pressure or find ourselves in a situation where we cannot find a way to resolve any problem, we become frustrated and mentally blocked.

In that case, we should take time to do breathing exercises.

As a result, we will have the ability to solve the problem that occurs at that time.

7. It is revitalizing

On the other hand, breathing exercises help revitalize us. To do this, we must accelerate the rhythm by inhaling and exhaling a little faster. At the end of the process, we must make some sound and even sing.

With this, we will be able to fill ourselves with energy and continue to be more active with daily activities.

8. Release the crying

There are times when we feel the need to cry, but that crying remains contained within us and represses us.

To exploit this feeling, we will take a deep breath with our hands on our chest, pretending to sob. We will see how, in a matter of seconds, we will be crying and draining that feeling that we had inside.

9. Full of energy

When we spend all day in the office in front of the computer, reading and writing reports or some other job, the moment comes when the dream attacks us.

Yawning and stretching the body on several occasions, we will be able to activate ourselves again and feel more awake to continue with our work. When we yawn, the mind fills up with oxygen and glucose, which are stimulants.

In short, breathing is not only a biological and natural function, but it also helps us to heal the soul in various ways. Therefore, let's begin to breathe consciously and achieve healing and better management of emotions.

CHAPTER 5

BREATHING TECHNIQUES TO REDUCE BLOOD PRESSURE

Breathing techniques can contribute to well-being. Therefore, it is worth learning and applying them when we have high blood pressure.

High blood pressure is one of the most common silent diseases in the population worldwide, and it is essential to pay attention to it once the diagnosis is indicated in the medical consultation.

When the doctor diagnoses us with hypertension, it is vital that we learn to take care of our diet, that we reduce the consumption of salt, and that we avoid a sedentary lifestyle.

But in addition to this, we must follow their treatment and recommendations, as these will help us enjoy a good quality of life.

Now, what if we had at our disposal one more strategy to reduce high blood pressure at home?

We talk about the always recommended breathing techniques, those aimed at reducing the heart rate through deeper and slower breathing.

Breathing techniques are complementary strategies for the treatment indicated by the doctor. Learning them can take some time, but in the end, they are very useful.

1. Focus on one word and breathe

A simple and effective technique to reduce blood pressure is to focus attention on one word, to focus on it to "turn off" mental noise as well as erratic thoughts that often cause stress or anxiety. Once we have reached that inner calm, we will begin the breathing technique.

We explain now how to do it:

- Sit in a comfortable place with your back straight.
- Choose a word: wind, forest, river, sun, rain, harmony, balance, peace, tranquility, flow, etc.

- Repeat it slowly until an image appears in your mind.
- Now take a deep breath.
- Hold that air for 4 seconds, then exhale loudly and for several seconds.

2. Breathing technique to "cool" the body

The proposal that we explain below may be curious but, still, it is useful and effective to reduce heart rate, calm the mind, and regulate blood pressure.

This technique is usually practiced in yoga and is called Sheetali, a term that comes from Sanskrit and could be translated as cold calm or cool the body.

We explain how to carry it out:

- Sit with your spine upright.
- Relax your shoulders and arms.
- Inhale air slowly, relaxed.
- Then stick your tongue out and, with the tip of it, trie to draw a "U" in the air.
- While doing this exercise, inhale for 5 seconds (concentration should be maximum).
- Now, quietly close your mouth again and perceive that curious freshness inside you

3. Reduce your high blood pressure in 5 minutes

This is a simple and effective option to harmonize our breathing and find mental calm.

Take note of the process:

- Sit comfortably, with your back straight.
- Then gently tilt your head back.
- Close your eyes and rest your hands on your knees.
- Now inhale and exhale five times, slowly, as slowly as possible.
- The breaths must be loud, so don't hesitate to pursue your lips as if you were going to pronounce the vowel "o."

4. Abdominal breathing

The breathing abdominal or diaphragmatic is the most known and certainly the most widely used. So, if we had to choose any of these five techniques to reduce our blood pressure, this would be one of the most useful.

Take note of how to carry it out.

- Place one hand on your chest and one on your belly.
- Now, breathe deeply through your nose, so that you perceive how your diaphragm is widening - not your chest.
- Hold that oxygen for a few seconds and then exhale deeply.
- Repeat it over 10 minutes, and you will see how your mind clears and your heart balances.

5. Alternative nasal breathing

We have already talked about this technique in our space once: it is useful to reduce stress and even to sleep better.

We recommend that you carry it out when you are in bed and 30 minutes before going to bed: it will provide you with a restful rest, and you will wake up with adequate blood pressure.

These are the steps you should follow:

- Sit comfortably, but with a straight back.
- Relax for a few minutes.
- Next, bring your right thumb up to your nose to cover the right nostril.
- Take a deep breath through the left nostril.
- When you've reached your peak of inhalation and can't breathe anymore, close the left nostril with your right ring finger.
- Now exhale through the other hole, the one in the right nostril.
- Then we do the same thing again, but on this side, that is, once we have taken the maximum air in that right nostril, we close it and exhale the air from the left.

CHAPTER 6

EFFECTS OF BREATHING ON THE BRAIN

Breathing more calmly and deeply can help you reduce feelings of stress or anxiety, even improve concentration.

The brain is one of the most important organs of our body and, in turn, one of the most sensitive. It is subject to all the changes that take place in our body, such as glucose levels, heart rate, etc. Hence the effect of respiration on the brain is also very important.

Breathing is the process by which we obtain oxygen and remove carbon dioxide through our lungs. Oxygen is essential for all reactions that allow us to live and function properly.

It is an automated mechanism. This means that, normally, we do it unconsciously, without paying attention to how we do it. However, we can consciously control our breathing.

The effects of respiration on the brain have been investigated in recent years. By knowing them, they have been able to develop breathing techniques that can help us in many aspects of our lives. In this chapter, we explain it to you.

What effects does breathing have on the brain?

For centuries, especially in the eastern areas, much importance has been given to breathing. It has become the protagonist of meditation techniques and different disciplines, such as yoga.

The effects of breathing on the brain were unknown until relatively recently. Research conducted at Stanford University has shown that the relationship between respiration and relaxation is scientifically based on brain mechanisms.

Although deep breathing is indeed recommended to deal with stress or panic until now, the mechanism by which this occurred was unknown. This research demonstrated the existence of a special group of neurons in the brain.

It is about 350 neurons distributed by the central nervous system. What makes them different from the rest is that they become more activated the faster the breath is. This is important because these neurons send stimuli to other parts of the brain.

Those areas are related to the feeling of panic, stress, and sleep. Therefore, one of the effects of breathing on the brain is directly related to these sensations.

What is the implication of this?

This effect of respiration on the brain allows us to analyze our respiration and adapt it to each moment of our life. As we have already mentioned, breathing slowly and calmly would activate these neurons less.

In this way, we could reduce our stress and anxiety levels. Even handle panic situations much more effectively. This breathing is called controlled, rhythmic, or deep. It is based on breathing with the diaphragm instead of mobilizing the chest.

This is what it's about practicing in both yoga and meditation. Breathing techniques for childbirth have also been developed to better cope with the moment of giving birth.

On the other hand, we can also use this effect of breathing on the brain in the other direction. We can breathe faster and more agitated to activate ourselves. Although, logically, there are more applications to seek calm.

Like any other tissue in our body, the brain needs oxygen to carry out its functions. However, the latest research has shown that there is another effect of breathing on the brain.

It has been shown that certain neurons are activated more when we breathe faster. They are related to stress and fear levels. Therefore, controlling our breathing can be a weapon to face our day to day.

It is necessary to learn to control breathing. For this, there are many people specialized or who know certain arts, such as meditation, in which this is a fundamental aspect.

The idea is to be aware of the importance of our breathing in the brain. Also, look at the way we breathe and practice deeper and slower breathing. Maybe this can help you noticeably control your emotions.

Controlled Breathing

Breathing is not enough. We will explain the characteristics of controlled breathing, and we will teach you how to use it.

Controlled breathing brings respiratory processes to our conscious sphere and allows us to observe their characteristics: rhythm, cadence, and depth. We train ourselves to know how to carry it out and modify it to achieve the objectives that we set ourselves.

Breathing is normally an automatic act that the brain controls and modulates through the brain stem without our conscious intervention. Many factors influence it in our emotional and psychological sphere. Furthermore, it is a source of information for our endocrine system in regards to the stress hormones secreted in the adrenal glands.

The characteristics of controlled breathing bring us multiple benefits, some of an immediate nature. Before going on to explain how to do it, let's do a brief review of the respiratory processes.

Breathing physiology

The function of the respiratory system is twofold. On the one hand, it must conduct the inspired air to the pulmonary alveoli, where the oxygen it contains will pass into the blood, and, in turn, collect carbon dioxide or CO_2, the product of cellular metabolism, to evacuate it through expiration. To the exterior.

This mechanism allows cells to convert carbohydrates, fats, and proteins into energy for their proper functioning.

Subsystems of the breathing process

- **Conduction system:** formed by the nose, nasopharynx, larynx, trachea, main bronchi, secondary bronchi, and terminal bronchioles. It is the area through which the passage of air to the lungs is verified.
- **Respiratory system:** it is made up of the alveolar sacs, the alveolar membrane, and the arterial and venous capillaries. In this area, gas exchange is carried out, collecting CO_2 from the arterial capillaries and giving O_2 to the venous capillaries.

- **Muscular system:** referred to the muscles involved in breathing. The most important is the diaphragm, although the intercostal and clavicular muscles also intervene to a lesser extent.

The circulatory mechanism of respiration requires that blood containing carbon dioxide CO_2 reaches the pulmonary capillaries, and this can be released into the alveolar sacs. The greater the blood flow, the greater the gas exchange takes place.

Since the circulation starts from the right ventricle, less muscular and powerful compared to the left, most of the blood flow is directed to the bases of the lungs, which, paradoxically, is the area that we ventilate the worst and with which we breathe the worst.

Types of breathing

Considering the location of the breath, we can divide it into abdominal or diaphragmatic, thoracic, or costal and clavicular.

Abdominal or diaphragmatic breathing

In this type of breathing, the diaphragm descends, leaving room for the bases of the lungs to expand their capacity. It is the most effective, and yet the least used breath.

Chest breathing

In thoracic respiration, the rib cage exerts a brake, marks a limit to the central expansion of the lungs, and is therefore not as effective as the abdominal one.

Clavicular breathing

It is the least effective. We can say that it is residual respiration because it covers the smallest area of the lungs, and its expansion mechanism is very limited.

Controlled breathing allows the full utilization of all types of breathing. It bases its functionality on abdominal breathing, makes maximum use of thoracic breathing capacity, and does not neglect clavicular breathing, despite its little influence on the respiratory process.

We will now detail what controlled breathing consists of its characteristics, and how to do it.

Characteristics of controlled breathing

Controlled breathing allows us to be aware that we are breathing, which is the basis of how to do it. Therefore we can vary its characteristics and train them on how to do it. We become aware of the respiratory process and influence its cadence, rhythm, and depth, adapting it to our greatest benefit.

In controlled breathing, we perform between 8 and 12 breaths per minute. It is a calm breath that allows air to be distributed throughout the lung and facilitates gas exchange through the capillaries.

In addition to these benefits, it affects and modulates stress activation mechanisms through the endocrine system and the sympathetic nervous system.

Unconsciously, the mind associates rapid, shallow breathing with a hazard that threatens the person and thus triggers the stress mechanisms through the release of cortisol by the adrenal glands.

Breathing, fast and shallow, is what we see in people who are going through extremely serious illnesses. It has been called the "intensive care unit breathing." This type of superficial and rapid breathing acidifies the internal environment and has negative consequences at the physical and brain level, complicating the prognosis of patients.

When we establish controlled breathing, we can vary the pattern of frequency and depth, going to moderately deep and slow breathing that is interpreted by our subconscious as a state of calm and peace.

With moderately deep and slow breathing, endocrine processes are triggered that remove stress hormones (cortisol and adrenaline, fundamentally) and stimulate the production of endorphins and the so-called 'happiness hormones': dopamine and serotonin.

How to perform controlled breathing

In the beginning, to properly perform controlled breathing, we will need to put all our conscious attention. With practice, it will become a habit, and you will only become aware in times of stress, anxiety, fear, etc.

Technique To Perform Controlled Breathing
Position

- Sit comfortably with your eyes closed.
- Place the palm of the right hand on the abdomen and the left on the chest.
- If the posture is uncomfortable, you can do the exercise standing or lying down.

Breathing

Breathe in and breathe out through your nose. If there is any difficulty, it can be done by mouth, but it is less advisable.

Take a slow breath in trying to direct it to the abdomen to notice how it rises with inspiration and falls with expiration. We will notice that the right hand will move rhythmically as the air enters and leaves.

We take air while we count to 3 and we expel it also counting to 3. At first, it requires our full attention, and it can be difficult, but little by little, it is done more easily.

You can count 1 when you finish inspiring by holding the air and then expire.

It is convenient to adopt the rhythm of the breath so that it is comfortable, slower, or faster, depending on our feeling of well-being.

To integrate the technique, once we have practiced several times, we can introduce variants. We can do the same exercises standing up without activity or doing something, doing it in bed before sleeping, or just after waking up.

When we already have some skills, we can increase the depth of breathing and the duration of breaks after inspiration and expiration.

Some Benefits Of Controlled Breathing

Physical

- It improves metabolism performance: increased energy and vitality.
- It facilitates the oxygenation of the body and, above all, of the mind.
- It reduces muscle tension, general pain, and migraines.
- It stimulates sleep reconciliation and reduces fatigue.
- It enhances the physical performance and functions of the immune system.

Mental

- It increases self-esteem and stimulates decision making.
- It improves concentration and performance.
- Strengthens emotional balance and enhances creativity.
- It helps disperse negative thinking and rumination.
- Facilitates relaxation and sleep reconciliation.

Other benefits affect the emotional, spiritual, and social dimensions. We can conclude that the knowledge of the process of breathing and the application of controlled breathing will improve many aspects of our life and, above all, it will raise our energy levels and well-being.

CHAPTER 7

HOW TO DO BREATHING EXERCISES TO IMPROVE SLEEP

Sleep disorders directly affect our daily life. There are many techniques and mechanisms to deal with them. Among them are breathing exercises.

Traditionally sheep have been mentally counted to sleep, but we can learn how to do breathing exercises to have a better quality of sleep. In this way, we will maintain proper sleep hygiene to avoid insomnia, the most common of sleep disorders.

Sleep hygiene

Today's dynamic world, loaded with stress and technological devices, increases anxiety and depression exponentially. The tranquility recedes, and insomnia appears at night. Likewise, alcoholic intoxication or excess caffeine is harmful.

Loss of sleep greatly affects health. It decreases performance, increases tiredness, and symptoms appear that can trigger serious pathologies. Immune, endocrine damage, sexual dysfunction, irritability, loss of concentration, or memory can manifest.

Fortunately, countering these types of symptoms is possible. We only need to learn a series of breathing exercises to have a better quality of sleep.

Turn off the TV and phone

Before starting, it is essential to check the conditions of the room. It must be dark, orderly, and silent. Let's move the alarm clock away from our field of vision since it can increase anxiety and obsession with falling asleep.

It is essential to turn off the TV and the mobile, also the light. This will help the body get ready to rest. Sleeping with the air conditioning on is also unhealthy.

An important recommendation is not to drink fluids before sleeping, as the desire to go to the bathroom will interrupt the rest. We will not bring pending work or a to-do list to bed the next day.

Getting up in the sunlight resets the biological clock. If possible, take an hour of the morning sun, ideal for people with sleeping problems.

Breathing exercises to have a better quality of sleep

Several exercises will help us counteract the stress that daily activity imposes on us. It is a matter of taking a few minutes to breathe, relax, and oxygenate the body and brain.

Diaphragmatic breathing

The most recommended by specialists is diaphragmatic or abdominal breathing. It improves metabolism, attention, and channel stress. It benefits the immune system, digestion, sex, and reproduction. Also, the abdominal muscles are strengthened.

Human beings get used to breathing with the upper part of the lungs. But when we take the air to the stomach, we learn to feel our body, and we are more aware of the moment. We also increase relaxation.

The recommended exercise to strengthen diaphragmatic breathing can be done lying down or sitting with your back straight. We place one hand on the chest and the other on the stomach, inhale through the nose and exhale through the mouth. The stomach must swell, and the chest does not move.

This type of breathing is also ideal for combating work stress. Three diaphragmatic or abdominal breaths, during which we relax our shoulders, neck, and forehead, will be enough to make us feel better. The brain works more relaxed, and productivity increases.

Concentrated breathing

Lying on our backs and with our attention focused on breathing, we inhale deeply through the nose. We hold three seconds and exhale through the mouth. We repeat the exercise eight times, resting five minutes in between.

Square breath

It consists of taking inspiration through the nose while we count to four. We retain the air, also counting to four, says that we will repeat while exhaling through the mouth. We count to four again while we are not breathing and repeat eight times.

4-7-8

Counting the breath times will evade us from external problems.

We part our lips and expel all the air. We close our mouths and inhale through our nose while we count to four. The count will be up to seven while we keep the air retained.

We part our lips and count to eight as we exhale through the mouth, slowly but with a hissing sound. The exercise is repeated four times.

Alternate nasal breathing

We cross our legs and place our left hand on the knee. We completely expel the air from the lungs and abdomen. With the right thumb, we close the nostril on the same side and inhale through the left.

Subsequently, we open the right and exhale through it. This rotation is maintained for five minutes and culminates by exhaling through the left nostril.

To control panic attacks

The ideal exercise to counteract panic attacks is to inhale for six seconds and exhale for another six seconds for one minute. Then we retain the air for 10 seconds and start the cycle again until the crisis disappears.

When you learn how to do breathing exercises to have a better quality of sleep, insomnia gradually disappears. The rest will be much more pleasant and therapeutic. In turn, it will improve body well-being, and with it, your quality of life.

Mindfulness Exercises To Sleep Better

One of the basic mindfulness exercises is to pay attention to breathing and listen to the sounds around us, but without trying to identify or filter them.

Mindfulness is a technique that has been integrated into medicine and Western psychology in recent years. It is used to reduce stress, increase self-awareness, and reduce stress-related symptoms, both physical and psychological.

All this is achieved through simple exercises that are capable of paying full and conscious attention to the experiences of each moment from interest, curiosity, and acceptance.

Among the benefits of mindfulness is the fact that you can sleep better since it optimizes the quality of rest in adults who suffer from certain types of moderate sleep disorder. Through mindfulness, a program is established that will modify the routines before going to bed, and that will make you sleep much better.

You must learn to make time for yourself. And it is that there are people who live stressed and finding 5 minutes a day, to connect with their interior, can be difficult. However, investing 10, 15, or 20 minutes a day for your well-being is not so much. Keep it in mind and put it into practice in your daily routine through these simple recommendations.

And it is that when it comes to mindfulness, the important thing, regardless of the techniques used, is to adopt the appropriate attitude. The one that promotes attention in the present moment, without judgment, and with compassion for oneself and others.

Only in this way will we get in tune with what is happening within us and around us. In turn, we will have the ability to unmask automatisms, and we will be able to promote integral development.

5 Mindfulness Exercises

1. Breathing is the key

Learning to breathe properly is one of the keys to achieving fullness. For this, you can look for some breathing techniques.

You will see how practicing five minutes of deep or complete breathing can make a big difference between the quality of sleep you had before and the one you can have now.

2. Do what helps you feel good

It is essential that you know yourself well and knows what to do to feel better and completely relaxed.

From listening to a song, watching a video, remembering a happy moment, walking for a bit of exercise, we can do a lot to distract ourselves, and we don't need to spend too much time on it.

Simply enough to give a new perspective to our feelings will be enough for you to relax.

3. Make a body scanner

With this simple exercise, you will come into contact with the experience of our body as it is, without judging, without rejecting unpleasant sensations or sticking to pleasant ones.

This exercise also called body scan or body scan, and to do this, and you need to sit in a comfortable position:

- It will be enough for you to have your back straight, although it is also possible to adopt the lying position.
- Then close your eyes, pay attention to your breath, and take a tour of the body.
- Surely you will notice the difference instantly.

4. Do it from morning

To start the day away from stress, you need to sit in a quiet place and turn off the TV so that you are silent. You must also have the phone away. It's about having no distractions: when you are about to have breakfast, try to focus your attention on the flavors, smells, the touch of food, or drink... Feel them!

In this way, you will be with attention in the present moment, and you will see the difference. Doing a little mindfulness from the morning will be a great help.

5. Be aware of the sounds that are produced at that moment

It consists of paying attention in a conscious way to the sounds that occur to our environment, and that is to stay very attentive.

Hear them as they sound, without trying to identify them, without judging them as pleasant or unpleasant, or thinking about them. Without any effort, the sounds are observed, and other external perceptions are set aside.

When noticing a distraction, we observe what it is that caught our attention, and we return to listening to the sounds. We rely exclusively on the breath of that moment. It is an exercise par excellence within mindfulness.

Finally, we hope that these tips have been useful to you and that you put them into practice. Rest assured that they will bring you great benefits.

5 Aspects Related To Poor Sleep Hygiene

For our body and mind to rest properly, it is essential to take care of sleep hygiene. We explain how to make it the most suitable.

We call sleep hygiene the control of all those behavioral, psychological, and environmental factors that prevent us from having a deep and restful sleep.

Even though we have all experienced what it is like to spend a few days in which we can't sleep in a restful and healing way, some people end up suffering from chronic insomnia due to certain behaviors related to poor sleep hygiene.

Nor can we forget that not resting, not enjoying deep and restful sleep, in turn, causes metabolic changes in our body that can lead to more serious diseases. We explain it to you below.

Insomnia affects our physical and emotional health

Our daily behaviors, including emotional ones, can have a major impact on our hours of rest. An example of this would undoubtedly be stress.

All that tension accumulated during the day tends to overexcite our brain, preventing us from reaching those deeper stages of sleep where our mind, our body, rests.

However, let us briefly see what the consequences of not enjoying adequate sleep hygiene are.

If we consider that we spend about a third of our lives sleeping, we can undoubtedly understand the great importance of promoting adequate rest. In the case of not achieving it, we can experience the following:

The body is not properly cleaned or regenerated.

We do not activate the production of certain hormones that promote the recovery of tissues and muscles.

According to various studies, insomnia breaks our glucose levels, and we are at risk of diabetes.

Our memory begins to fail, and it is difficult for us to concentrate, to solve problems. It can even change our mood.

Increased stress from chronic insomnia can increase the risk of heart disease. It's something to consider.

Factors that determine poor sleep hygiene

1. Go to bed angry or worried

Something that usually happens many times at the couple level, for example, is waiting late in the day to talk about those problems or those issues that worry or bother us.

Getting to the pillow after a couple's argument prevents us from getting a good night's sleep. The same thing happens when we make use of this moment when we turn off the light, to "spin" certain complicated events of the day related to work, family, emotions...

The most appropriate thing is that two hours before going to bed, we have solved or addressed those problems that worry or bother us. We must be aware that the pillow is rested and light of negative emotions.

It is difficult to achieve, we know, but it must be encouraged.

2. Don't go to bed hungry or "too full"

Sometimes we choose not to eat dinner to lose weight. Also, and on the opposite side, some make a hearty dinner and come to bed just as digestion is taking place. None of this is healthy.

We have to eat two hours before going to sleep, and dinner should be varied, fair, but always nutritious.

Do not consume exciting or alcoholic drinks, also remember that certain infusions such as tea can activate us. An ideal remedy to relax would be to have a glass of almond milk with honey, delicious.

3. The bedroom should be dark and at a temperature between 18º and 22º

A messy bedroom with an unpleasant odor and a high ambient temperature is synonymous with poor sleep hygiene. It will undoubtedly be very difficult to get a restful sleep.

The room should be dark or in a warm half-light. The scent of lavender, for example, is very relaxing.

The ideal temperature with which to get a good night's sleep is between 18 and 22 degrees.

4. Be regular in your habits

Very classic bad sleep hygiene is to go to sleep every day at one hour and get up at another. Hence, when, for example, working several shifts, our physical and emotional health suffers, by altering our circadian rhythms.

Try, as far as possible, to synchronize your habits with the sunny hours. In this way, we will regulate the release of melatonin to promote adequate rest.

Another aspect that we must remember is the one referring to the use of mobiles, computers, tablets. All of this also affects our melatonin, hinders its function, and overexcites our brain. The most suitable thing would be to close them two hours before sleeping and take a book.

5. Don't exercise just before going to bed

Whoever says physical exercise can also refer to tasks such as cleaning the house, putting washing machines, walking the dog. Everything that involves exercising our body just before going to sleep also means poor sleep hygiene.

Try to complete these tasks at least an hour before bed. When you're done, take a hot shower, have a glass of warm honey milk, grab a good book, and release all kinds of worry from your mind.

Rest, sleep will embrace you slowly and deeply.

Four strange symptoms of stress and four quick strategies to cope with them

CHAPTER 8

HOW INCORRECT BREATHING CAN AFFECT YOUR HEALTH

Did you know that, in addition to influencing performance, the type of breathing is also related to weight gain and the ability to activate the feeling of satiety? We tell you how inadequate breathing can affect you.

Breathing is an essentially biological process for life and, although we do it automatically, many times, we make some mistakes that can affect health. What are the consequences of incorrect breathing?

It is important to note that by breathing, we inhale not only the necessary oxygen for the body but also particles and chemicals that seep into the respiratory system. Also, it should be considered that this action is key for the functioning of the heart, the lungs, the production of energy, and the physical state in general.

Because of this, it is essential to identify what type of breathing is performed and what are the effects on health. Besides, it is convenient to learn to do it correctly to avoid negative consequences in the medium and long term.

What are the consequences of incorrect breathing?

The negative consequences of incorrect breathing are numerous since its function is linked to the work of the other body systems. It mainly affects the digestive, nervous, cardiovascular, and muscular apparatus; However, it has a lot to do with the emotional state.

Some of the health problems caused by this inappropriate action are:

- Depression and anxiety.
- Chronic fatigue.
- Digestive diseases.
- Increased risk of cardiovascular accidents.
- The weakening of the immune system.
- Increased blood pressure and heart rate.
- Asthma or choking symptoms.

- Neck and shoulder strain.
- Lack of concentration and memory loss.

Breathe through the mouth

Breathing through the mouth is one of the most frequent mistakes. Experts warn that this habit has negative consequences on phonation, swallowing, and even body posture.

By using the mouth instead of the nose to breathe, the action of filtering and warming air from the nostrils is prevented. This leads to the development of health disorders like pharyngitis.

Whether caused by hypertrophy — enlarged tonsils or adenoids — or changes in the internal anatomy of the nose — septum deviation or turbinate hypertrophy — this type of breathing causes abnormalities in the face and the entire dentofacial region. In turn, these problems compromise the ability to chew and the aesthetics of the smile.

Bad breath and obesity

Bad breath is associated with people suffering from obesity. This is because several factors undermine its efficiency, as the brain loses the ability to activate the satiety mechanism in time.

On the other hand, this disorder plays an important role in the sleep and oxygenation of the body, which has a lot to do with body mass. Excess weight implies a greater effort to breathe, which increases the tendency to breathe more through the mouth than through the nose.

This leads to sleep apnea, snoring, and other nighttime disorders, which in turn greatly increase the risk of weight gain.

Impaired oxygenation

Another factor derived from inadequate breathing that must be considered is the poor oxygenation suffered by the tissues. By failing to get the necessary amount of oxygen to the cells, serious problems arise for the nervous system, brain health, and the digestive mechanism.

This lack of oxygen also affects other vital organs, as well as skin, hair, and nails. For all this, doctors advise doing breathing exercises that allow improving the technique. With this, errors are corrected, and the brain is restored to the innate way of doing a good breath.

How to breathe correctly?

Correct breathing is done with the lower abdomen area. When inhaling, this area expands outward and laterally, while when exhaling the stomach can be slightly towards the center.

On the other hand, it should be borne in mind that between 6 and 10 breaths are made per minute. This frequency varies depending on the person's age, physical condition, or emotions, among other factors.

The main benefits of adopting good breathing are:

- Better oxygenation of cells and tissues.
- Less cardiac effort.
- Less tiredness and muscle tension.
- Reduction of stress and anxiety.
- Greater physical and mental performance.
- More lung capacity.
- Increased exercise tolerance.
- Less risk of respiratory and heart conditions.
- Vagus nerve activation and nervousness control.

Do you feel identified with the problems derived from incorrect breathing that we mention here? Take action and train a few minutes a day with a proper breathing technique and check that it has a lot to do with the state of your body.

Relieve Back Pain With A Simple Breathing Technique

It is recommended to perform this technique twice a day. If we do the second before bedtime, it will help us feel more relaxed and fall asleep more deeply.

Is it possible to relieve back pain through a breathing technique? If you are one of those people who suffer from this ailment, you may be surprised.

Back pain is usually relieved after taking a pain reliever or an anti-inflammatory. Massages from a physiotherapy specialist are also very effective in these cases. Now, could a breathing technique perhaps do that too?

It is known, for example, that yoga is very therapeutic for all those who suffer from back pain.

Exercising our body by practicing certain stretches and using our breathing, always manages to relieve pain and offer us a little more mobility.

In this chapter, we are going to talk about a technique developed by Andrew Weill, director of medicine at the University of Arizona (United States), that helps us to alleviate this type of frequent ailments.

It is simple, inexpensive, and non-invasive, so do you join us in this simple breathing exercise?

Can Breathing Relieve Back Pain?

Before teaching you how this breathing technique works, we want to delve a little into the question of whether it can be effective or not, taking into account the opinion of the experts:

- From the Avanfi Institute of Traumatology and Physiotherapy in Madrid (Spain), they explain to us that the human body has a muscle called "transverse abdomen." Its purpose is to offer stability in the area between the back, abdomen, and pelvis.
- It is like a kind of belt that surrounds us from the navel to the spine.
- This muscle aims to offer stability in our posture and, in turn, protect the back.
- This muscle oppresses the viscera of our abdomen, so that, each time we breathe, it exerts a movement of "fixation" to the back and throughout our interior. It is a structure in turn that is part of the exhalation of air during breathing.

While moderate exercise and breathing techniques are effective in relieving back pain, it is also interesting to learn more natural alternatives to alleviate suffering.

Breathing can relieve back pain

Whenever we carry out a type of slow breathing, we will exercise the movement and resistance of this central muscle of our abdomen, which goes from the navel to the spine, and we will be able to relieve back pain.

The secret is in knowing how to exhale, that is, in expelling the air, at which moment that muscle moves. Now, we have to release all the air to the maximum, until we notice that it oppresses us.

The contraction of this muscle is very effective in protecting the lower back.

Technique 4-7-8 to relieve back pain

Previous aspects that you should take into account

This exercise will have more effect as we practice it more frequently. That is, the first day will relax you, the second will make you feel rested and lighter and, on the third, you will notice a clear decrease in back pain.

You must practice it every day. Do not take more than 5 minutes.

Never repeat it more than twice a day. It is very appropriate that you do the second before sleeping. This will help you feel more relaxed and fall asleep more deeply.

How to Perform the 4-7-8 Technique to Relieve Back Pain

- Wear comfortable clothes that do not oppress you.
- Sit in a place with a firm base where you can also lay your back comfortably.
- Close your mouth and inhale deeply through your nose for 4 seconds.
- Now hold your breath for 7 seconds.
- Now you must exhale (blow out) that air from your lungs for 8 seconds. You already know that this is the most important part, there where we exercise the back muscle of the abdomen, and that will help us to alleviate back pain.

- Repeat it four times (two sessions a day).

Other tips, relaxation techniques, and exercises that may be useful to us

- Meditation to control stress and anxiety.
- Yoga or tai chi is suitable for relieving back pain.
- The swimming.
- He walks every day for half an hour.
- Do not hold the same positions for a long time.
- Don't bend your back when you have to pick something up from the floor: bend your knees.
- The mattress of your bed should not be too hard or too soft; it should adapt to your movements, with a low pillow and bedding that does not weigh.
- Never sleep on your stomach, as it will force you to bend your head to breathe, and you will get neck and back pain. The best posture? In the fetal position.
- Never carry too much weight in your bags.
- Avoid being overweight.
- Always avoid self-medication. It is usual that before back pain, we immediately resort to anti-inflammatories, which can bring us various side effects.

In the event of any discomfort, go to a professional to explain the origin of this ailment. Follow their advice and always remember to maintain good postural hygiene when you are working or even at this very moment when you are reading the article on your mobile or laptop. How are you sitting?

CHAPTER 9

HEALING TECHNIQUES THAT BRING YOU MENTAL BALANCE

Since concerns affect all parts of our lives, to achieve well-being, it is essential to achieve a mental balance that helps us overcome difficulties.

The mental balance in a human being is linked to the state of harmony existing between body, mind, and spirit. It mainly depends on the use of energy from thought and the acts or actions that result from it.

A person is said to have a good balance when he can control his life. This balance also helps strengthen the immune system. If a person focuses their energy positively on their daily activities, it will make them sick less often.

To help you, we leave you some techniques that will allow you to achieve this balance easily. Get down to business and be happier.

1. Music therapy

Music has been shown to influence health and peace of mind. Furthermore, music can improve learning and concentration processes since it stimulates and activates the brain.

Instrumental, classical, and harmonious music can benefit the body and promote a mental balance in the human being. However, any type of music will be of great help to you.

Choose your favorite rhythm and take the time to listen to it for a few minutes a day.

2. Intrapersonal psychology or introspection

Strengthening our mental state and our emotions through self-reflection or introspection is very useful when finding mental balance.

In this case, we talk about the self-knowledge that you generate about yourself. Through this exercise, you can strengthen your values, feelings, perception of life, and even overcome the fear of death. This can be done through self-help reading or personal writing.

3. Psychotherapy

If you find intrapersonal psychology somewhat difficult, we recommend opting for psychotherapy.

This is to unburden or heal any kind of memory or emotion that does not allow you to find the expected mental balance. It can also help you improve your quality of life by modifying your behavior, feelings, or thoughts.

4. Relaxation

Some relaxation techniques, such as yoga, allow us to get a deeper rest of our mind. These techniques decrease exhaustion and allow you to increase your energy levels, optimism, emotional, and mental stability.

From all this, it follows that relaxation is a technique of mental balance that also helps to promote your spiritual and physical well-being.

5. Meditation

The use of meditation through breathing exercises, object-centered attention, and the use of sounds has been very useful in improving memory. In case the above does not surprise you, you should know that it also helps reduce stress, improve mental and physical health.

Meditation has been used in many cases to treat various psychological disorders. We recommend you try it as a complement to other techniques that we have mentioned.

6. Reading

We talked earlier about how self-help reading can benefit mental balance. However, reading in general, done in a quiet or open space, also favors your mental health. In addition to exercising the brain, it allows you to develop thinking skills. It also influences your ability to organize and focus.

7. Neurofeedback

Through technological advances, it has also been possible to treat stress, depression, or anxiety. The neurofeedback is a computerized technique that monitors brain waves of the patient using electrodes placed on the surface of the skull.

Through different computerized procedures, the individual is made to learn to control his behavior and influences his mental well-being. This is a very advanced technique and can only be applied under the supervision of a professional.

Work on your mental balance in a reasoned way

Finding mental balance is a very personal task, and we do not always attach importance to it. However, it will give you enormous benefits if you pay a little attention to it.

If you have been through a situation of emotional difficulty or feel that your life is not going well, stop for a moment to work on your mental health. You can do this by reserving a few minutes a day or committing to therapy; you choose how, but do it.

Remember that anyone's ultimate great goal should be to achieve happiness and fulfillment.

How To Breathe Correctly When Swimming

Learning to have good breathing while swimming allows you to perform better during swimming exercises. Besides, it prevents the feeling of fatigue and some muscle tension.

Maintaining proper breathing when swimming is one of the keys to improving performance and preventing that uncomfortable feeling of fatigue in the water. Although it is a bit tedious at first to have good coordination when breathing, you can master it with practice.

The problem is that not everyone spends time on breathing techniques and ignores those mistakes that accelerate tiredness. Also, some become accustomed to holding the air for long stretches, ignoring that said action lowers the heart rate. Fortunately, the tips for correct breathing when swimming are not a big deal. Are you interested in learning about them?

Tips for maintaining correct breathing when swimming

When practicing swimming, it is important to have well-prepared lungs. However, the technique for correct breathing when swimming may vary depending on the type of swim. In general, the goal of mastering it is to optimize the performance of the exercises, since a soft and relaxed breath saves valuable energy.

Bilateral crawl breathing

The key to correct breathing when swimming in the crawl is to do it bilaterally. This technique requires the swimmer to change the side he breathes on after each full stroke cycle. Its alternation can occur every 3 or 5 strokes.

Benefits

- Decreases the tension in the shoulder area.
- Improves balance and body alignment.
- Contributes to greater energy savings.
- Enhances location ability and helps control vision on both sides.

Butterfly style front breath

In the butterfly style, it is easier to breathe. To do it correctly, the swimmer must breathe forward, keeping the head as high as possible. That is, it takes air when the head is removed and expels it when it returns to the water.

One of the variants that are currently being used is the fact of breathing every two arms cycles. This is called "respiration rate 2 and 1" and is used to achieve better performance.

Back-style breathing

Many feel comfortable when swimming in the back style since breathing is much easier than in other modalities. However, trusting is not advisable, as the swimmer may lose control of the posture and swallow water.

To avoid any inconvenience, it is essential to watch the rhythms and coordination, trying to inspire the air before the arm crosses the vertical of the head. A common mistake is to take and sun air continuously, without considering the body's movement when swimming.

Reverse breathing

In swimming, breathing is done on the contrary. The air is taken in through the mouth and expelled through the nose. This tip is essential to have correct breathing when swimming since it helps it to be more efficient. The expulsion of air through the nose allows more controlled breathing since all the oxygen is not released at once. Therefore, it stays in the lungs longer and prevents that feeling of suffocation.

Consequences of bad breath when swimming

Failure to breathe correctly when swimming has several negative consequences. Although sometimes they are not perceived in the learning process, over time, they become an obstacle to achieving optimal performance. The most commons are:

- Greater resistance to advance because the hips and feet tend to submerge more than they should.
- Feeling of fatigue because it increases the need to make unnecessary movements.
- Lack of general oxygen throughout the body, which increases premature tiredness.
- Dizziness when there is a breath in each stroke.
- Drowning sensation when holding your breath for a long time.
- Exhaustion and muscle tension due to overstrain.

How to breathe correctly when swimming

Are you worried about having bad breath when swimming? Take into account the recommendations given for each case, but assume them naturally. Do your normal swimming exercises, but focus on having better breathing. In this way you will make it increasingly spontaneous and, also, you will improve your performance. If you have doubts or feel that you are doing it wrong, ask for the supervision of a coach.

CHAPTER 10

BREATHING TECHNIQUES FOR LABOR

Breathing techniques during labor vary according to the rate of contractions and timing. We tell you in detail what they consist of and how they help.

Breathing techniques during labor give a lot to talk about today. They have become one of the essential pillars in preparation for when the time comes for delivery.

Breathing techniques are known to help the mother cope with childbirth. They activate the circulatory system and contribute to maintaining the muscular effort. They even relieve pain that, as we well know, is very intense.

Moreover, these techniques also improve the baby's oxygenation. It's about taking deep breaths at a steady rate. In this chapter, we explain what these techniques are so that you are prepared when giving birth.

How do breathing techniques for labor help?

Maintaining deep, rhythmic breathing during labor has many benefits. This is backed by scientific evidence. For example, a study published in the Journal of Integrative Medicine concludes that:

"Deep inhalation and exhalation breathing exercises in pregnant women are effective in reducing the perception of labor pain and shortening the duration of the second stage of labor."

They are also related to a reduction in the number of assisted deliveries. This has a simple explanation. Due to the feeling of tension and pain, breathing tends to become fast and shallow. This reduces the amount of oxygen you inhale and bring it to the baby. It also causes your muscles to work less forcefully.

Knowing breathing techniques that help you face this moment of fear and tension allows your breathing to be deeper. By getting the right amount of oxygen, you will reduce the risk of complications for your baby.

What breathing techniques are used?

The fundamental pillar of these techniques is to inspire through the nose constantly. You have to do it calmly. Then you must expel the air through your mouth without pressing your lips together. It is very important not to hold your breath during labor.

It is necessary to consider that the breathing techniques are changing as the labor progresses. Therefore, we will now explain how this sequence occurs.

Start of labor

This is the time when the contractions start, but they are still quite long apart and not as fast. In this phase, slow or abdominal breathing is usually used:

- This technique involves gently inhaling air through the nose while the abdomen swells.
- Then it tries to expel the air, slower than inhalation, through the mouth. Try to breathe out three times more than you inspired.
- Between one breath and another, the idea is to take a short pause. This breathing technique helps manage the rhythm of contractions and relieve pain.

Progress of contractions

As contractions increase, the best technique is light accelerated breathing. In this phase, it is completely normal for breathing to accelerate.

This technique is based on inhaling more briefly. However, it is necessary to continue doing the same: the air is taken in through the nose and is expelled through the mouth.

You should try to breathe in a little air when the contraction begins. Then try to breathe it out when the contraction ends. You can do this in several expulsions or just one.

During this phase, chest-level breaths are usually done, since it takes more time to maintain the baby's oxygen levels (and his own!).

The final moment

When the time comes to deliver the baby, the breathing technique that is often used is called the expulsion breath.

- It involves inhaling a large amount of air until you have the feeling of having filled the lungs.
- When the urge to push is very strong, you should tilt your chin toward your chest. When you push, you let the air out little by little. Every time this happens, repeat the technique.
- Ideally, between effort and effort, you breathe naturally to recover.

Breathing techniques for labor are very helpful as they help relieve pain and deal with contractions with force and energy. It is normal for you to be afraid that the time is coming and to be afraid of forgetting these birth preparations.

However, preparation courses and midwives make it possible for these techniques to be almost intuitive during childbirth. However, try to practice these techniques before the time comes.

Techniques To Relieve Labor Pain

It is inevitable to experience pain in childbirth. However, before it is time to give birth, the mother can practice some relaxation techniques to make the symptoms more bearable.

Labor pains are one of the biggest fears of all pregnant women. Although the sensation is subjective and varies from woman to woman, in general, it is characterized by intense pain with each contraction. Applying techniques to relieve labor pain is very productive.

Fortunately, several methods promote pain relief, and that not only provides a greater sense of tranquility but prepares the body for when it is time to give birth.

How do techniques to relieve labor pain work?

When it is time to give birth, contractions occur. In this process, the upper part of the uterus contracts and the lower part stretches and relaxes to facilitate the movement of the baby through the birth canal.

Due to pain, a woman tends to contract and tighten her entire body each time she has a contraction. Although it is a natural response of the body, the tension is exhausting and can prolong labor by reducing the effectiveness of contractions.

For this reason, some relaxation techniques have been incorporated into labor for many years. Its main objective is that, while the uterus undergoes contractions, the future mother releases the rest of the body from tension and controls her anxiety.

Although there is not yet a scientific basis that these methods can reduce pain, their relaxing effects are beneficial. However, it is important to practice them from a little before the "big day" to have a better effect.

1. Accompaniment during labor

Mothers who choose a trusted person to accompany them in labor feel more well-being and relaxation. That company could minimize the need for interventions such as cesarean sections. Or the use of epidural anesthesia.

2. Freedom of movement

One of the techniques to alleviate labor pain is to have freedom of posture and movement while the time comes. Lying in bed is not always the best way to minimize tension, and waiting still can be even more stressful.

Therefore, during contractions in the first phase of labor, it is appropriate to walk or make some kind of movement. This increases the release of endorphins and promotes well-being.

Also, activities such as pelvic rocking favor the opening of the cervix and the passage of the baby.

3. Breathing exercises

Breathing exercises are included in many of the childbirth preparation classes. This type of technique allows mitigating the pain of contractions in the active dilatation phase. Also, it helps the mother to focus on keeping a rhythm and listening to her body.

Among other things, slow, deep breathing significantly reduces muscle tension and provides peace of mind. That is why, from the beginning to the end of the labor process, it is good to practice it.

4. Listen to music

Thanks to its therapeutic effects, listening to music can serve as one of the techniques to relieve labor pain. Choosing relaxing melodies, for example, to accompany the breath, releases the tensions and fears typical of this process.

With soft melodies, the perception of pain is reduced, and the stress caused by contractions is mitigated. If the delivery is in the hospital, it would be good for the companion to carry some songs prepared for the mother to relax before giving birth.

5. Bathtub with hot water

Waterbirth is one of the best-known methods to alleviate pain. Contact of the body with hot water produces a strong sensation of relaxation on the muscles and joints, reducing ailments.

Likewise, it reduces the segregation of adrenaline and favors the softening of the cervix. For this reason, more and more hospitals are adapting rooms with bathtubs for those who want to have this type of experience. Also, the mother can choose whether to give birth in the water or not.

Although there is no method that 100% eliminates labor pains, the practice of these simple techniques can minimize them so that the moment is not so traumatic.

The constant support of the couple or a family member, as well as breathing and massages, can make these feelings more bearable.

Prenatal Stimulation Techniques

Prenatal stimulation techniques allow you to connect with your baby while she is in the womb and awaken her senses. There is no scientific evidence that they stimulate intelligence or learning.

Every pregnant woman has spent many minutes stroking her bulging abdomen, trying to figure out if she is touching her baby's foot, elbow, or knee. That is the first and most intuitive of the prenatal stimulation techniques that every woman does.

There is no scientific evidence to indicate that prenatal stimulation techniques affect the baby's intelligence or learning ability. However, the truth is that they are exercises that can be very pleasant for the mother and open ways to strengthen the bond with her child.

How to apply prenatal stimulation techniques?

There are exercises for each stage of your baby's growth. To follow any of these techniques, the most important thing is not to obsess. Along with the stimulation moments, there also have to be quiet moments.

The fetus inside the uterus also sleeps, and since we don't know when it does, it is better not to abuse with excessive stimulation.

Visual stimulation techniques

It is known that starting from the sixth month, the fetus reacts by opening and closing its eyes to light stimuli that come through the abdomen. Therefore, you can start these exercises from the fourth month:

- Uncover your belly in sunlight 20 seconds and then cover it for 20 seconds.
- With a small flashlight, light your belly and move slowly from top to bottom or from one side to another.

Tactile stimulation techniques

Pressing the abdomen generates vibrations that are transmitted through the amniotic fluid, and your baby feels them through his skin. These exercises can be performed from the tenth week of gestation.

If there has been previous abdominal pain, miscarriage, or premature labor, it is best to refrain from doing these exercises.

- Press on the abdomen area or give a very light blow when you feel the baby's movement.
- At the time of showering, drop water with different intensity on your belly.
- Gently massage your belly or ask your partner to do it.

Auditory stimulation techniques

The baby hears many sounds inside the uterus: your heartbeat, digestion, or breathing. He can also perceive what comes from outside, your voice, and that of Dad, even though the amniotic fluid dampens the intensity.

Still, it is important to avoid arguments during pregnancy because your baby feels what is happening. You can start these exercises from the fourth month of gestation.

- Select a piece of music, preferably instrumental, and listen to it relatively frequently.
- Speak to him in a strong, leisurely voice and get your partner involved too.
- Sing him a lullaby, which you will then return to sleep once he is born.

Motor stimulation techniques

Being in smooth but rhythmic motion helps both mother and baby. It relaxes you and helps you stay fit throughout your pregnancy. For the baby, it is a different way of perceiving the outside world.

These prenatal stimulation techniques can be started after the fifth month of pregnancy. If you are going to perform them, you must have the consent of your doctor, since if you have had a threat of miscarriage, you must take care of yourself.

- Dance gently, alone or with your partner.
- Swim or walk regularly.
- Practice yoga or Pilates prenatally.

Mental stimulation technique

Focusing attention on what every inch of the body feels helps to release stress and tension. Body scanning is a simple technique, although it takes some time to master.

You can do it anytime, anywhere. Lying or sitting, whichever is easier according to the volume of your abdomen:

- Start with what you feel on your toes, concentrating your breath and attention on that feeling.
- Thus, it covers the foot, ankle, calf, knee, thigh, and hip. Go to the other foot.
- After returning to the pelvis, continue with your back, belly, chest, shoulders, arms, hands, neck, and head.

Be aware of every sensation. If you feel your mind wandering a lot, become aware of it, and refocus on your breath.

It takes time to keep the focus on your body, but once you do, you will enjoy more of the process your body goes through during pregnancy and of your baby within you.

Your baby has developed his senses in the third month, so these exercises are ideal for the second and third trimester of pregnancy when the initial discomforts have passed. Just spend a couple of weekly sessions doing any of these prenatal stimulation techniques.

Important: do not obsess. Enjoy the opportunity to connect with your baby if your partner can get involved much better. If not, another family member can also participate. And, of course, if you have doubts, be sure to consult the doctor who follows your pregnancy.

CHAPTER 11

BREATHING EXERCISES FOR KIDS

Breathing exercises for children promote more optimal states of relaxation and concentration.

Children's breathing exercises are as useful as they are beneficial. Not only do they help them control their emotions much better, but they also improve their attention span: span and focus. Also, they feel more relaxed because they become more aware of their body, their processes even managing to improve their communication processes.

Also, more than one may ask the following question: Is it that children do not come into the world knowing how to breathe? It is clear that, yes, we all do it. The biomechanics of inspiration and expiration are automatic processes. Now, the question that should encourage us to a simple reflection is the following: we all know how to breathe, but do we do it well?

The answer is no. We don't always breathe correctly. To begin with, a more than evident fact is that we do not take advantage of all our lung capacity, we forget that we also have a diaphragm and that this can wonderfully optimize the entire process.

Likewise, another fact that we do not forget is that, on average, we breathe very fast, we take very little air with each inhalation, and this forces us to do it several times and in an arrhythmic way. All this translates into a greater feeling of tiredness, frequent headaches, and a greater impact of stress and anxiety on our body.

Now, in the case of babies, there is a curious fact that must be considered. When a child comes into the world, he breathes correctly, he breathes deeply and uses the diaphragm. However, as it grows, either by postures or by lifestyle, it loses that natural ability.

Teaching children how to breathe "well" through games will allow them to regain that forgotten ability to gain quality of life.

Breathing exercises for children

Studies like the one carried out at the University of Broadmeadow in Australia show us the physical and psychological benefits of deep breathing. Also, Daniel Goleman once explained in an article on how beneficial breathing exercises can be for children. He gave the example of a small school in Harlem, New York, and how a teacher had introduced the dynamics of "friends who breathe" into their classrooms.

The benefits of five minutes of deep breathing

1. Every morning, and before classes started, all those little ones between 5 and 6 years old would lie on some mats with a beer in their bellies.
2. They were to take a breath for 3 seconds and watch their favorite stuffed toy soar. Then they inhaled deeply and started again.
3. This game lasted just over 5 minutes, and yet something Daniel Goleman could see is that its effects were beneficial.
4. This exercise strengthened the brain circuits of the children to improve the processes of attention and emotional management.
5. Thus, those students who had been practicing these morning breathing sessions for more than two years showed fewer attention problems and hyperactivity as well as a greater disposition to study and learn.

As we can see, something as simple and elementary as dedicating a small interval per day to this series of breathing exercises can have a very positive impact on their development and abilities. It's worth a try.

1. The snake game

Simple, fun, and effective. The snake game is a favorite of the little ones and consists of the following.

How do we do it?

- We will seat the children in a chair, indicating that they should have a straight back.

- They should put their little hands on the abdomen and focus on the orders that we are going to give them.
- They should then take deep air through the nose for 4 seconds. We can count the time for them, noting in turn how their bellies swell.
- Then they must let go of that air while making the snake sound. It must be a hissing sound that will last as long as they can.

2. We are going to inflate a very large balloon

The second of the children's breathing exercises are just as entertaining. To do this, we will follow these steps.

How do we do it?

- The child should sit comfortably in a chair with a straight back.
- Now we will explain that the game consists of inflating an invisible balloon, a colored balloon that must be very, very large.
- To do this, they must take air through the nose and then exhale. They must imagine how it swells and how it gets bigger and bigger.

In this exercise, children (like adults) tend to catch air through their mouths. It is what we all do when inflating a balloon. Therefore, we must correct them and indicate that the nose catches the air while our belly swells. Then they should exhale, pursing their lips as if they had that giant colored balloon in their mouth.

3. Breathing like elephants

This breathing game is one of the most successful among the little ones, and they love it. The guidelines we will follow are as follows.

How is it done?

- Children should be standing with their legs slightly apart.

- We will indicate to them that they are going to become elephants and that they are going to breathe like them.
- They must take a deep breath through the nose, and when they do, they will raise their arms as if they were the animal's trunk, in turn trying to make the abdomen swell.
- Next, it's time to breathe out. To do this, they must do it through the mouth in a sound way and lowering the arms while they bend down a little, bringing the "elephant's trunk" down.

4. The leopard's breath

The last of the breathing exercises for children is somewhat more complex but equally fun and effective in getting them started on diaphragmatic breathing.

How is it done?

- We will instruct the little ones to get down on the ground on all fours like a leopard.
- Now they must take a breath through the nose, noticing how the abdomen swells and the spine descends.
- Now they must exhale through the mouth, perceiving in turn how the abdomen empties and the back rises a little.

Note that this exercise is worth doing slowly so that children perceive these processes in their bodies related to this type of breathing, which, in essence, is the most beneficial.

Point out that there are many more breathing exercises for children within our reach, it s enough just to find those that you like the most and with those that correctly perform each step to make them a daily routine. Only in this way will they learn to breathe better, only in this way will we enhance their development and their quality of life a little more.

Relaxation Exercises For Children

Playing is part of the child's comprehensive development. The little ones have to run, jump, dance, tinker, and move. However, sometimes they need to relax and be calmer. We propose a series of relaxation exercises for children that will undoubtedly benefit their physical and mental health.

Through these techniques, they will be able to reduce their anxiety, stress, insomnia, and they will be able to control their emotions and behaviors better. Besides, they will make your mood improve. Best of all, achieving this calm state does not have to be boring, but can be achieved by uniting the two domains. Welcome to playful relaxation.

Jacobson and Schultz methods

Jacobson's is one of the most widely used methods in the world. It is based on the contraction and subsequent relaxation of different muscles or muscle groups.

Simply by lying down on the floor, we can indicate to the child what parts of the body he has to tense for seconds. And then relax. Thus, the child will notice a progressive relief that will spread throughout his body. We can start with individual muscle groups like the hand or the neck. And then increase the difficulty as you get to practice.

For its part, the autogenous method of Schultz is one of the relaxation exercises for children that can be used from approximately six years of age. The technique is divided into two levels: the lower and the upper, and is based on the sensations of heaviness and heat.

Reclining on the floor, the child is asked to focus on those areas of the body that he feels weigh the most (legs or arms) and keep more temperature. Once you stop appreciating them like this and consider yourself free of tension and burden, we can do it with other upper body parts of the body. Thus, we gradually relax all the muscles.

To make it easier for you to follow the instructions, we may urge you to think that at first, it is like a robot. Therefore, it has to move like a stick and only by rigid movements. Then, to relax, he turns into a rag doll, where his body is soft and lacks muscle tension.

Rejoue's game

Rejoue's game is one of the most fun. In French rejoue means replay, so let's put it into practice!

This method proposes that the essence of life is made up of pairs of opposites. Thus, we find cold-heat, day-night, up-down, black-white, activity-rest... Hence, this technique brings together relaxation exercises for children based on those pairs.

To do this, rocking is used a lot, which consists of imitating the movement that a rocking chair does. Thus, the child starts almost all the muscle groups to swing back, forth, to one side and the other. This duality occurs when, on the one hand, the child has to tense some parts of his body, but on the other hand, he must free others from that tension. Only this laxity will allow you to perform the balance well.

Another game is stretching. Children are taught to differentiate between the sensation of stretching and relaxing. For example, you are asked to open your arms and stretch them as far as possible to all sides. You must hold that position for a couple of seconds. Then they are asked to relax them gently. They will feel a tickle after doing it several times.

Peer Activities

Sometimes children scamper behind each other, and it is difficult to calm them down. And much more complicated is that they can stay focused after those moments of excitement. Therefore, the activity of the feather duster can be a good ally in these cases.

Its execution is very simple. It consists of playing relaxing music in the background and dividing the classroom into pairs. One of its members lies on the floor, while the other strokes the body with a feather to the music. And then the position is changed.

Similar to this is the softball game that is also done in pairs. A child lies on the floor with his eyes closed. And the other, to the rhythm of the music, is massaging his partner's body with a small ball. As if I were lathering it.

Viewing nice images

If there is one skill in which children are truly privileged, it is imagination. They are so free and innocent that we can almost afford any license to relax them. In this sense, a good way to achieve calm is through visualization.

To do this, lie on the floor and focus on your breathing for a couple of minutes. Next, they are asked to focus on what we are telling them aloud. We ask you to imagine a large, greenfield, a quiet and silent meadow with perfectly cut grass. We tell them to feel how that field smells, how the birds' sing, or the texture of the flowers.

The image display can have multiple applications and can be versioned with beach, mountain, or odor landscapes. As we see, the possibilities are as many as you have imagination. The main objective is to make children have fun playing relax.

That is, they do it without feeling that it is an obligation. For this, it is convenient for the elderly to do the same as them. Remember that imitation is the main source of learning for children. Therefore, these relaxation exercises for children are also for adults, because it is always good to preserve innocence!

CHAPTER 12

RISK OF SUFFOCATION IN ROUTINE ACTIVITIES

Breathing is the natural process that allows you to inhale air to store some of its elements and then expel it. Temporary or permanent interruption of breathing is known as suffocation, which can be caused, among others, by choking on food, ingesting foreign objects, hanging by ropes, or by drowning in liquids. Among the consequences of suffocation is the temporary or permanent loss of motor and cognitive functions, or in the worst case, death.

There are people who, due to their special condition, are at high risk of suffocation in each of the activities they carry out or are exposed to daily. This is the case for babies and young children who have small airways and explore the world by putting objects in their mouths. Additionally, they have less practice controlling food in the mouth and do not have molars to grind them until they become a smooth paste. This risk of choking suffocation may be equal to or greater in disabled people or older adults, even more so if they have difficulty chewing or swallowing.

Some activities that go unnoticed are illustrated below. However, not infrequently, they have been related to suffocation deaths. Remember, Prevention Is Your Most Important Partner.

Bathing: At bath time, the child must be watched at all times. Neglecting the child in the bathtub or pool by answering a phone call or the doorbell can be the difference between life and death, even when the child has special chairs, floats, or mechanisms to prevent drowning.

Cleaning the home: An unexpected case of death when cleaning the home occurs when the child manages to get into the bucket of water that is being used to mop and falls headfirst into it. Due to the size of the bucket, the child, and the position in which it falls into the bucket, the minor can't get out, and he suffocates in a few minutes. The same happens when a child manages to climb a toilet or a pool. Never leave objects that make it easier for a child to climb them.

Do not leave buckets unattended even if they contain very little water. In the same way, when lowering the ropes of the clotheslines, you must verify that the children are not playing in the vicinity, these ropes have also become a death trap in which the children die by hanging.

Looking out the window: An activity as innocent as looking out the window has taken the lives of children who have become entangled in the ropes of the blinds that allow them to make a loop that ends around the children's neck. This type of hanging has also occurred when the cribs are left close to the strings of the blinds or curtains, and babies or children play with them.

Play: Small parts that come off toys, such as a car wheel, a teddy bear's eye, or part of a sticker, can block your airways and cause suffocation, just like playing with a bag that used as a toy packaging. Cords used to pull a toy, when too long, have also caused hangings in infants and young children. Be careful not to leave only children in the presence of small parts and buy only toys certified with a security seal.

Play in the park: Some clothing items have cords to provide a better fit at the waist or on the face, as is the case with hoods. These ropes can get caught in railings or runways and cause suffocation or strangulation death. The same can happen with other clothing like scarves or superhero costumes that have capes.

Transportation: When children get out of the vehicles and close the doors, the same ropes or clothes just mentioned can get caught and drag the child when the vehicle starts. The consequences can only be limited to blows and fractures, but the risk of suffocation also occurs in these cases.

Play in kindergarten: Again, the combination of the rolling pin and the rope used for a girl to carry her student card were the cause of her death as the rope became entangled when the girl slipped down the rolling pin.

Eating: Numerous deaths have been reported related to different types of treats that slide easily into children's mouths, as well as foods such as sausages, nuts, mamoncillos, grapes, raw vegetables, jellies such as peanut butter and rosettes of corn among others.

In general, any food that is slippery and difficult to control in the mouth, or that its size or consistency can cause respiratory blockages, should always be administered in small pieces or quantities, especially to children under the age of four who at their young age they do not master the ability to chew, which can lead to them being able to swallow whole foods.

Additionally, you should not promote laughter or talk while eating, or walk, play, or run with food or eating utensils in your mouth. Always check the packaging of the goodies and carefully follow the instructions and warning notices.

Sleeping in the baby car: Two and a half million baby cars were removed from the market for the death of four babies who fell asleep when they slipped and fell through a hole in which their neck was stuck, preventing breathing. When purchasing a baby car, check that it does not contain holes in which your baby can be trapped and never leave your child unattended.

Sleeping in bed with parents: Bed-sharing is the most common cause of death in babies less than three months old. Keep your baby's crib next to his bed so he can be close to him at night. The American Academy of Pediatrics (AAP) advises sharing a room with your baby, but never a bed.

Sleeping in the crib: Mattresses that do not fit the size of the crib perfectly or leave gaps between the two are another potential cause of suffocation risk. The same goes for items such as padded crib bumpers that are not properly attached or that loosen threads where the baby can tangle their neck. Do not put padded protectors, loose bedding, toys, or other soft objects in the crib that could put your baby in danger of being trapped, strangled, or suffocated. Do not put him to sleep on a water bed, sofa, soft mattress, or another soft surface. Portable bed rails don't always prevent the baby from rolling and falling out of bed, and babies can get stuck in them and hang themselves.

Halloween: Masks that are not provided with specially designed breathing holes and make it difficult to remove from the head because they are held by ropes that are tied to the child's neck, are an imminent danger of suffocation, which also happens with the ropes used to tie the layers of superhero costumes to the neck. Always check that the mask is provided with breathing holes, that it is easy to remove by children, and prefers layers that have "easy removal" systems.

At home: Different studies have shown that three out of ten children aspire or ingest Foreign Bodies (CE), which corresponds to one of the main preventable causes of death in children under three years of age.

One of the studies presented was carried out in the Garrahan, Gutiérrez and Alassia pediatric hospitals from January 2010 to April 2012, in which it was detected that the highest incidence occurs in children under three years of age with 52.2% of cases—analyzed, while the group of children between 6 and 14 years old represented 23.4%. In 80.3% of the events, there was an adult present at the time of the accident that occurred while the child ate (48.13%) or played (39.33%).

Children up to 3 years of age are the prevalent victims due to curiosity, exploration of the environment through the mouth, immature swallowing, children's propensity for distraction, playing while eating, and lack of ability to distinguish objects—edibles of which they are not.

Choking is the fourth leading cause of accidental death in children under the age of five, according to the New York State Department of Health. The United States Consumer Product Safety Commissions (CPSC) reports that about 15 deaths from suffocation are recorded each year in children under the age of 3 and warns: "Food, toys, household items and basically any Anything that fits into your child's mouth is potential suffocation risks."

If you notice any of the signs of suffocation such as inability to speak, wide-eyed panic look, difficulty breathing or noisy breathing, inability to cough loudly, skin, lips, or nails that start to turn bluish or blackish or loss of consciousness and you have the training to Assist a suffocation victim by giving him five blows on the back and five chest compressions, do it immediately. Continue until the choking object is expelled, and the baby, child, or person may cough loudly, speak or breathe, or until you become unconscious, in which case you should require specialized medical help. If you do not have the training indicated above, apply repeated abdominal compressions (known as the Heimlich maneuver) until the object causing the suffocation is expelled and the person can cough loudly.

Remember. The Superintendence of Industry and Commerce is vigilant and vigilant so that these consumer accidents do not occur. If you are aware of a product that, due to its specific characteristics, may hurt health, integrity, or life, under normal circumstances of use, contact the authority immediately. Your complaint helps save lives.

CHAPTER 13

HOW TO BREATHE TO CLEAR NEGATIVE EMOTIONS AND MEDITATE

As you well know, the act of breathing is essential to oxygenating the cells of our body and, therefore, to stay alive.

But breathing also has other functions and uses, such as clearing negative emotions, balancing the solar plexus, and preparing the body and mind for meditation. In this chapter, I will explain exactly how to achieve it. Let's start with it.

The importance of breathing

The act of breathing allows air to pass into the lungs so that the oxygen it contains can pass directly into the bloodstream and from there to every one of our cells. Without oxygen, our cells would die, and, therefore, breathing is essential to stay alive.

Breathing is possible thanks to the action of the diaphragm muscle, an anatomical structure located transversely between the chest and abdomen. The diaphragm is located precisely in the region of the solar plexus, just between the third and fourth chakra, the first being responsible for emotions. And it is also a place of passage for the main blood vessels of the body, as well as certain nerves of the autonomic nervous system that directly contact the spinal cord and the brain.

For all these reasons, when we breathe correctly, we help drain the large blood vessels and stimulate the nerves of the autonomic system, responsible, among other things, for regulating visceral dynamics, heartbeat, or breathing itself. That is why breathing well is synonymous with digesting food more efficiently, optimizing heart rate, and better oxygenating our cells. This contributes to improving the health of the body, but also of the mind since the neurons of the brain also require oxygen and nutrients to function optimally.

In short, a good breath will optimize not only bodily functions but also the mental ones, which helps us find the optimal balance point that allows us to connect with our Essence, regulate our emotions or meditate.

Meditative breathing

Meditation and breathing are two related parallel processes. Meditation requires a particular, slow, and deep breathing, while a good breath is in itself a technique that takes the person to mental and physical states of the meditative state.

Below I will explain how to breathe easily and effectively during our meditations:

To begin with, we will place ourselves in any sitting position that allows us to relax without risk of falling asleep, either in a chair or on the floor in the lotus position, and we will place the backs of our hands-on our thighs. From this position, we will take slow and deep breaths, trying to relax during each one of them gradually. The inspiration will be through the nose, while the expiration can be done interchangeably through the nose or the mouth. However, we must perform abdominal or diaphragmatic breathing, that is, inflating our abdomen during inspiration and deflating it during expiration while trying to make our chest move as little as possible.

Only with these simple respiratory instructions, we can correctly carry out our meditations. However, if our objective is to clear negative emotions and balance the solar plexus, we must introduce some variants to this technique and take into account some considerations.

How to breathe to clear negative emotions and balance the solar plexus

All emotions, even in a subtle way, can be perceived at the level of the solar plexus, that is, in the pit of the stomach, just behind the lower part of the sternum, where the third chakra is located, the emotional chakra. To clear negative emotion, it is not only necessary to know how to listen and interpret the sensations of the solar plexus and try to find the cause that generates it. It is also necessary to treat the bodily maladjustments that these emotions cause. The most common physical imbalance is a diaphragmatic spasm, which manifests itself in the form of anguish, a feeling of tightness in the chest, and rapid and shallow breathing, among other symptoms. If the diaphragmatic spasm is not released, these symptoms will persist over time, and, in the long run, the emotions that provoke them can reproduce even though we have treated their cause.

One of the simplest and most effective ways of treating diaphragm spasm is through breathing. By breathing correctly, we decrease the muscular tension of the diaphragm, and we managed to make it perform a gentle mechanical pumping on the nerve endings of the solar plexus and the anatomical regions of the third and fourth chakra. This will help regulate negative emotions that may originate at that level, and we will enter a calm and calm state of mind. At that time, we will obtain a relaxation of the general tone of our muscles and, therefore, an increase in the feeling of well-being. From this new situation of tranquility and physical-mental relaxation, we are more efficient when meditating or doing introspective work that allows us to identify and deal with the cause of our emotions.

The respiratory work proposal to achieve these objectives starts from the diaphragmatic respiration that is explained in the previous section. However, now we will be in a lying position on our back and with flexed legs, although eventually, it can also be done in a sitting or even standing position. In this case, the slow and deep breaths we were taking will be accompanied by inspiratory apneas. That is, at the end of each deep inspiration, we will pause for between four and ten seconds in which we will retain the air in our lungs.

It must be said that any relaxation technique we perform can be effective in achieving the same goals. Relaxation techniques often have one of their fundamental pillars in breathing, as they are a key factor in lowering muscle tone and reducing the activity of the central nervous system.

CHAPTER 14

HOW TO BETTER MANAGE ANGER BY BREATHING?

Continuation of the series on emotions. This time we will talk about anger. Anger is an emotion that will energize, often too much. This energy, when it is misdirected, will lead to behavior that is not reasoned or to store this energy in the body and block it. In either case, it is not an ideal way to manage anger. In this chapter, I will, therefore, give some solutions to better manage anger through breathing always!

Anger, a useful emotion?

What is anger for? Emotions are there to signal information to us. What brings anger? Why are we angry? Concretely, of all emotions, anger is the vainest emotion in terms of use. Admittedly it brings a surplus of energy which manifests itself in the form of overactivity or force in the best of cases. However, more often than not, it does nothing good in action.

So why get angry? To know what our place is. We are angry because we feel that something is not going the way it should be. So we can turn it all over the place; the source of the anger always comes from there.

This emotion is, therefore, interesting for structuring a hierarchy at a community level. Besides, it is anger that motivates social movements (at least those who make the social movement). But what does it teach us? To accept that we are not all-powerful and that we have no control over everything.

Limit anger by working on our prejudices or values

Before giving solutions to control anger, it seems important to offer something all the same to limit its appearance. It is impossible never to be angry. At best, we can delude ourselves that nothing puts us in this state, and we will repress this energy in the body.

One of my teachers said that depending on how we manage anger, and we will end up with a heart attack or cancer: infarction is for those who let the anger come out, cancer for those who keep it. We have no intention of getting there, and we will have solutions, but all that to say that it is not possible to escape from anger.

On the other hand, it is interesting to ask questions if you get angry all the time. At that time, there is a real problem to be resolved. Anger, as I said, happens when you feel that something in the universe is not happening as you think it should be. Frustration and intolerance for the latter is also a sign that your anger management is certainly poor.

If you are angry all the time, then you need to review your image of the universe and how it works. It is only you who can lower your scale of values so that it no longer triggers anger.

Be careful; I am not saying that you must leave your values aside, but more than that, you must manage the anger cursor associated with these values. Let's take an idiotic example. I feel that I am paying too much tax and that I should pay less. It's unfair, and it makes me angry. So every year I will be angry when I pay my taxes. However, I cannot help it, and there is a form of the inevitability of the thing. So, it is up to me to accept that it is like that, it is the functioning of my universe, I do not have any hold on it, so I don't have to get angry. On the other hand, if I have a hold on it and I have the power to change the thing, in this case, it is useless to get angry, I make a change what I dislike.

How to match our values and trigger anger

Decreasing the threshold for triggering anger is not easy. Already, because you have to accept that if you feel it, the problem comes from you and how you receive information.

Here is a fairly soft and simple protocol to start this work:

- Lie on your back and practice a natural breath of at least 4 seconds of inspiration and 4 seconds of expiration (find the rhythm on which you are comfortable)
- Remember the last time you got angry, keep your breathing in place
- Ask yourself what value in your home has been affected
- Then always look with the same breadth and the same rhythm for the times you got angry for this value
- If this happens often, ask yourself if you can change the situation once and for all.
- If yes do it
- Otherwise, keep breathing on the same rhythm and imagine that the situation is happening again and then accept the situation

- If your breathing rate changes, start again with a new situation impacting the same value until the situation no longer causes anger, and your breathing rate remains stable.

Your breathing, while you think, will be in control of the autonomic nervous system, which will have taken over. From an emotional point of view, no difference between reality and an imaginary situation. So if the situation causes anger, your nervous system will speed up your breathing, leaving you in no doubt. It is only when the situation will no longer cause it that breathing will remain calm. It is the beginning of work.

Note: that it is not because the situation does not trigger anger that it is a situation that you enjoy. However, it will no longer trigger a disproportionate emotional reaction.

Managing anger when it's there

Now let's see how to manage the anger that is there. The key is in the diffusion of energy. This is what we do naturally but not necessarily in the most intelligent way. The "con fracture" is the perfect illustration of this... But the idea is there.

Anger is an emotion that gives strength, and it gets lodged in the muscles. It is, therefore, necessary to evacuate it by movement. Here is the protocol that we will use:

- Take a full apnea, hold it for about fifteen seconds
- Exhale as strongly as possible
- Immediately after, do a series of ten rhythmic breathing squats
- Redo a fifteen-second apnea
- Exhale as strongly as possible
- Then do a series of ten rhythmic breathing pumps
- Finally, do one minute of explosive breathing, followed by one minute of rhythmic breathing.

At the end of this exercise, you should feel silent, and your body should not want to move. If not, repeat the cycle.

Cleanse the body

Last point, our body registers anger, more or less, depending on the character. It is good from time to time to relax the tissues with the following exercise to evacuate them:

- Lie on your back
- Star-stretch all of your limbs to the tips of your toes
- Inhale as much as possible then hold full apnea while trying to stretch even more
- then exhale, letting the pressure come out without blowing and relaxing completely
- Repeat this cycle three times.

Do this exercise several times a week.

Here are some tips for managing anger. The best is, of course, to modify in-depth what triggers it. However, keeping the body "clean" will not consume energy for nothing and will not be on edge, anger promoting anger. Try these exercises. Do them a lot at first and then as the mood stabilizes, slow down and stop.

From there, manage it on an ad hoc basis, when it appears. Remember, it's normal to feel angry, and you don't want to lose that emotion. It is, however, necessary that it does not eat your life!

CHAPTER 15

BREATHING EXERCISES TO IMPROVE CONCENTRATION

Concentration meditation on breathing, to be done before each practice, if possible.

Mental calm is essential to have clear ideas and appeased emotions.

Sometimes when we meditate on a subject, we do not succeed because our mind is too dispersed.

Before each practice, it may be good to perform this exercise, which calms the body, mind, and emotions.

Just be careful not to be surprised by the effects, because it is a powerful practice. but, suddenly, it helps for all the meditations that we do next, whether analytical meditations, concentration, or even mantras.

Also, it helps to concentrate energy in your body, which increases the effectiveness of your practices, whatever they are.

For this exercise, you need a little imagination and practice it enough the first few days to feel the effects (a 5/10 minute workout every day is more than enough, which counts being the regularity).

Exercise:

You settle down comfortably and stably (sitting, in lotus or half-lotus, or lying down, whatever), you try to become aware of your body, then you let your muscles relax gently, by releasing the pressure.

Then, we empty our lungs before starting the exercise, and we take a first abdominal breath, where we make the stomach swell well, for 3 seconds. The air we have just breathed in must appear pure to us, and do us good, and we imagine its journey to our feet.

We then block our breathing for 2 seconds, observing the air at our feet, and, then, we exhale for 5 seconds, and allowing the belly to deflate, and always observing the path of the air. This air remains in front of our noses, about 10 cm.

Then, we block our breathing again for 2 seconds, and we breathe in the same air again for 3 seconds, imagining that it goes to our feet, stays there for 2 seconds, then goes back to the nose for 5 seconds, there remain 2 seconds, then we breathe in the same air again.

After a few cycles, we will see the body calm down very powerfully, and our concentration will be much more intense.

This exercise is also very beneficial for people who would have concerns about heart palpitations and stress, but it is necessary to respect the cycle "3-2-5-2", and to breathe with the belly.

For this exercise to be the most beneficial for you, the best is to put your hands on your belly and to offer a slight resistance to inflation and deflation of your belly.

As with any meditation exercise, it requires a little practice before fully mastering it, but it is beneficial. Once we know how to do it properly, it is of great help in our practice, especially for the calm and focuses.

PS: If you follow the pattern and you feel like you're running out of the room, in two periods, you regain regular breathing ... But be alert, the inspiration will also be shorter than the deadline in order not to hyperventilate; this is very important; otherwise, you risk causing palpitations. Here are nine exercises to do before and during labor.

1. Focus on your breathing

Sitting or standing, with your back firmly seated on the seat or camped on your two legs, inhale and exhale at your normal rate ten times in succession, remaining attentive to your breath. You will bring your emotional state back to neutral.

2. Fix an object, just that object

Isolated in your office or while waiting for an interview, force yourself to "zoom" on an object, ideally neutral (not a photograph of a loved one or a holiday souvenir), like a notebook, a telephone, a chair, etc. .. Then for a minute, this. What one is long! Look at all the details, the contours, the shape, the sound, the scent, and do not make yourself care of anything else.

3. Fix the object, then its surroundings

As before, look at a single object but do not dwell on it. Fix it for 20 seconds and then widen the focal length, examine what surrounds it, the wall, the table on which it rests, the green plant next to it, etc. This gymnastics is effective as a preamble to all creative work. You thus have your mind to go beyond a specific point and to browse in unexpected corners that will facilitate associations of ideas, innovation.

4. Listening to music

For people sensitive to sounds, voices, this is an interesting help. There are two ways to use it:

- Listen to a song that will put you in the right emotional state for the situation. If you are going to perform soft cropping with a collaborator, choose a concerto. If you have to win a contract with a stubborn buyer, prefer rock.
- Isolate while listening to each of the instruments - piano, guitar, drums - one after the other. Your attention will be sharpened.

5. Counting in your head

7x2 = 14; 7x3 = 21; 7x4 = 28 ... Remember your multiplication tables, do mental math, subtraction, division, logical series of numbers. It is a really good method because this activity then monopolizes the brain. Only mechanical and repetitive gestures can be carried out simultaneously: pedaling on a bicycle, swimming, doing push-ups. Another advantage, the exercise is of elastic duration according to his mood.

6. Slow down your gestures

Make yourself an "open" bubble of concentration. That is to say, not closed to the world, on pain of experiencing the slightest question as aggression. Before a capital interview at 10 a.m. or writing a sensitive report, get up in the morning taking your time: dress slowly, enjoy the shower, allow yourself half an hour for breakfast and not 10 minutes, walk slowly, etc. You then enter the next phase, the senses on the watch, having saved your energy.

7. Identify your "attentional style."

Researcher Robert Nideffer, who is keen on sports psychology, found that the athlete's interest functions in two dimensions: reach (broad or narrow depending on whether it is based on one or more pieces of information) and orientation (internal or external depending on whether it is concentrated on thoughts and feelings or an external occurrence or object). Example for a footballer:

- Narrow internal: I mentally repeat a penalty.
- Narrow-wide: I visualize five passes on a field.
- External-narrow: I visualize the goal.
- External-large: I visualize the whole terrain.

8. Visualize the course of the action

This technique used by athletes before the competition works well before a public speaking, negotiation, or complex issue. It involves repeating the scene three or four times mentally in real-time and by viewing all the details (decor, atmosphere, microphone, or another tool) and all the steps until final success.

A leader feared that he would be destabilized during an assembly by critics of his peers on his social and environmental policy. He watched the film in his head and was able to develop replicas. On D-Day, at the dreaded moment, he was able to assert himself by staying in his subject.

9. Find your switch and activate it

During the short mental film described above (or by exploring your past), identify a sensory stimulus that connects you to memories linked to success. A kind of "off"/"on" switch, called "switch" by sports coaches, which immediately soothes and triggers positive energy and maximum concentration.

CHAPTER 16

ARE YOU AWARE OF YOUR BREATHING?

We breathe since we are born. The act of breathing is an act of life in itself. However, most of the time, we do it on autopilot, not using one of the most valuable tools we have to improve our physical and emotional well-being.

Breathing is synonymous with life. The act of breathing is part of our existence from the first breath at birth to the last one that takes life. We breathe automatically, but it is also one of the basic physiological processes over which we have, also, some control. But how many times a day are you aware of your breathing?

Becoming aware of breathing is the first step in learning to pay attention to it. Thus we manage to fix the mind and immediately stop all the thoughts we deal with at the same time, as well as the annoying internal dialogue. But there is much more. By becoming aware of your breathing, you can, in turn, manage and direct it.

Incorrect breathing can cause tiredness, depression, or anxiety. Conscious breathing can solve these problems and revert them to a healthier mental and physical state. Numerous conscious breathing techniques give us new control over our minds and the modification of thoughts and emotional states. These techniques are often used in therapy. Let's see some.

Mindful of your breathing: some guidelines

Our breathing varies depending on the activity we are doing or the emotional state we have. When we do conscious breathing, the first effect is that there is control over thoughts that, in turn, influence emotions. When it comes to becoming aware of your breathing and practicing any of the techniques, it is best not to exceed 30 minutes of daily practice.

Conscious breathing is always done through the nose, both inhaling and exhaling. When the technique requires slow breaths, this is not negotiable. There is a belief that a high level of oxygen in the blood is healthy, but it is not. The objective is to maintain correct cell oxygenation and that the level of CO_2 in the blood is indicated for its normal vasodilatory functions.

This is what is achieved with conscious breathing when performed slowly. Otherwise, we hyperventilate, and the CO_2 in the blood decreases, and the blood vessels constrict, which is the case with holotropic respiration. The latter must always be carried out with the help of a professional.

Slow abdominal breathing

If we observe our breathing, we will realize that in many cases, the air we inhale only expands the upper part of the lungs. If we look at a baby, we will see that the air he inhales swells his tummy. Over time, we tend to lose that kind of calm, deep breathing. Regaining abdominal breathing is the goal of this technique.

By making the air reach the abdomen, noticing how it swells, what we are doing is using all the lung capacity; we bring air to the lowest part of the lungs.

It is very important to do it slowly. Counting to five when inhaling and again five when exhaling is an adequate rhythm. It is the simplest technique to start making you aware of your breathing and is also indicated to reduce anxiety.

Retention techniques

In this practice, you must take a deep inhalation, retain the air in the lungs for the time that passes while we count to ten, and then release the air very slowly. This technique is widely used to discharge tension.

Reverse retention breathing consists of doing ten slow breathing exercises, expelling on the eleventh exhalation all the air that we are capable of; The lungs are then kept empty for as long as possible, to inhale normally again. This exercise is completed 10-15 times. It is indicated for insomnia problems.

The technique of increased respiratory rate

This technique has variants, but basically, it consists of achieving a respiratory cycle of 2 seconds, 1 to inhale, and 1 to exhale. It is used briefly and in cases where we feel out of energy, and an increase in vitality is required. It is the respiratory substitute for the stimulating effect of coffee, for example.

The most fun variant is doing this type of breathing while mentally visualizing that laziness and apathy are discharged with each exhalation. People should avoid this technique with a tendency to anxiety or with high blood pressure problems because it increases the heart rate. It is also recommended to do it at first under supervision.

Managing Emotions Through Breathing

The body, emotions, and thoughts form a whole. What happens in each of these areas has effects on the others.

There is not the slightest possibility that they will act separately. Hence, when you are in trouble, it is convenient to ask yourself not only for one of those components but for all of them.

One of the functions that have the greatest impact on physical and mental health is breathing. At the same time, breathing reflects emotions, feelings, the relationship with the environment, and the general state of the body.

Therefore, learning to breathe can help you significantly to manage your emotions better.

Breathing in emotions

Breathing is part of the body's autonomous system. The functions that make up that system, for example, digestion, operate without our command.

However, breathing is the only activity in that category over which we can exercise a significant margin of control. Hence we can learn to manage our breathing for our well-being.

Breathing changes according to the emotion that prevails in our minds. When we feel fear, it becomes more difficult to breathe, and it is as if we ran out of air.

Choking sensations may appear. If there is anxiety, breathing becomes fast and extra, so there is not adequate oxygenation of the brain.

If sadness predominates, breathing becomes much slower and deeper. Hence, it is not uncommon for sighs to appear very frequently in depressed states. In stressful situations, breathing becomes ragged.

When breathing changes its regular function, all the vital rhythms of the body are also altered. That is why it is so important.

Breath management

To learn to manage emotions through breathing, the first thing you should know is that this function can be of various types. There are two ways of breathing that affect the emotional world:

- **Abdominal breathing.** It is the natural way of breathing; that's why babies have it at birth. In this type of breathing, it is as if you swallowed the air and carried it to the stomach. It is based on the operation of the diaphragm.

Abdominal breathing is highly healthy to relieve tension and oxygenate vital organs such as the heart and liver. If you practice it frequently, you get great benefits.

- **Energetic breathing.** It is the one that appears during the moments in which we perform physical exercises. Its main function is to fill the organism as a whole with vitality.

Energetic breathing is very suitable for moments of great emotional difficulties since it fills us with vitality.

How to manage anger through breathing?

Anger is an emotion most harmful to the body and mind. So you must learn to control it, to avoid greater evils. You can do it through breathing.

The moment you experience anger, stay still. Then breathe in deeply and then breathe out, with all the force you are capable of.

Anger is like a pressure cooker about to explode; breathing with great power, is similar to the release of pressure in these types of devices. If there is no such escape, there will surely be an explosion.

When you experience some exhaustion in breathing, begin to inhale and exhale slowly. You're already calm.

By using breathing, you avoid an emotional overload that could harm your organism, and you also avoided a probably unnecessary conflict.

Evaluate the way you breathe daily and become aware of what she reflects. By taking care of your breathing, you also protect your body, your mind, your life.

CHAPTER 17

BREATHE WELL, BREATHE CLEAN

Without air, there is no life. Our first food upon arrival in this world is taken through breathing. It is the first thing we do for ourselves at birth: breathing, our first source of energy. And exhaling is the last thing we do just before we die. Air is our gaseous food and respiration, one of the best tools that we can use to balance our body, our mind, and our general health.

However, we seldom stop to think about the importance of breathing in our lives. If we pay attention to the purely physical aspect, how we breathe is of great importance for the state of our internal organs, which depend on the oxygen of the blood. With an inhalation, we oxygenate every cell in our body, and with an exhalation, we help detoxify the body (that among many other things). Hence the enormous importance of the quality of the air we breathe.

According to the World Health Organization (WHO), air pollution currently poses the greatest environmental health risk. It is responsible for the premature death of about 7 million people each year from diseases such as cancer, strokes, heart, and lung diseases. Also, last year the "First World Conference on Air Pollution and Health took place" And in t, countries and organizations made more than 70 commitments to improve air quality. The burning of fossil fuels (oil, coal, gas) is one of the main causes of pollution. At the administration level, much work remains to be done. Still, individually we cannot look the other way, and it is necessary to become aware of our responsibility as consumers and of the importance of the quality of the air we breathe for our health.

Breathing connects us with ourselves but also with others and with the planet. To raise awareness of this, since 2004, the "World Breathing Day" has been celebrated, which last year changed its annual date to April 11 and its name to "World Day of Conscious Breathing." The "International Breathwork Foundation" promoted the celebration of this day, an international network created in 1994, which brings together professionals, organizations, schools, and all those interested in working with the breath. Its objective is to spread among individuals, professionals, and institutions, what is optimal and conscious breathing, and to remind us of the basic and vital importance for future generations of clean and healthy air and environment.

Conscious breathing as a therapeutic tool

Throughout history, different cultures have had schools with conscious breathing techniques: India, China, Egypt, Persia, Greece, Rome and many of them included forms of conscious breathing as an integral part of their system of medicine. The Tibetan, the Chinese, and the Hindu are the most widespread in the world and the most widely practiced today.

There is an intimate relationship between moods and the type of breath, while each type of breath allows us to recreate a mood. When our mind is calm, breathing is slow. In the same way, if we attend to our breathing and make it slow, our mind will relax. So it is important to pay attention to how we breathe. It is the so-called conscious breathing, which not only helps us to make the energy flow balanced through our body, but also relaxes the mind, reduces anxiety, improves mood, increases vitality, and even helps us with good digestion and better assimilation of nutrients.

Breathing As Gaseous Food

If we look at food holistically, that is, as a whole, we see that our body feeds on the air we breathe, liquids, and solids that we ingest regularly. They are the three ways in which we find matter in the universe; all essential for the functioning of our physical body, from lowest to highest density, we have gaseous, liquid, and solid food.

As gaseous food, we have the air we breathe. The respiratory process is vital since, without breathing, our body dies within minutes. The air is composed of a chemical composition mainly of Nitrogen and Oxygen, although also in smaller proportions we find Water vapor, Carbon Dioxide, Methane, Helium, Hydrogen, Ozone. In addition to substances such as pollen, dust, volcanic ash and other components air quality pollutants such as mercury, sulfur, fluorine, or chlorine.

We must breathe through the nose, as long as there are no difficulties that prevent it, such as problems with the nostrils, mucus, being a smoker ..., since we have natural filters that prevent the entry of dust and hostile organisms such as bacteria and viruses. It also regulates the temperature and humidity of the air that enters our lungs. When inhaling, air enters the lungs, reaching the blood oxygen and traveling to the cells. These consume Oxygen during the process of making energy for our body and dispose of Carbon Dioxide, which in turn will do the same way but in reverse. From the cells, it passes into the blood, reaches the lungs, and returns to the air through respiration. We do this process without thinking and unconsciously almost always.

Paying attention during the day to how we breathe and how it affects our body gives us multiple physical and energy benefits. It is the so-called conscious breathing, and it not only helps us to make the energy flow balanced through our body, but it also relaxes, reduces anxiety, increases vitality, improves mood and even if we do it during meals, it helps with good digestion and better assimilation of nutrients.

A good exercise to become aware of breathing is as follows:

- Breathe in deeply and slowly through your nose
- Keep the air in the lungs for a few seconds
- Exhale through the nose releasing the air as slowly as possible
- Keep the lungs airless for a few seconds
- Start the cycle again and repeat the actions several times

Breathing also has therapeutic uses through various and multiple types of exercises based on the same points explained but varying the residence time in each of the phases of the cycle (seconds clear). These exercises serve to calm, purify, tone, balance, maintain and increase lung capacity, help in respiratory diseases, maintain the muscles in general, slow the progression of diseases.

An important factor to consider when breathing consciously is the ionization of the air. Ionization is a natural, physical, or chemical process by which ions are produced. Ions are molecules or atoms that contain an electric charge called an electron. Depending on the number of electrons gained or lost, ions are positive or negative. But now is not the time to do a physics class, so I'll get to the point.

The ionization that brings benefits to the human body is negative and is the one that helps us breathe better and more deeply. In contrast, positive ionization can be harmful to humans.

In nature, ionization processes are constant, for example, positive ions are formed when different atmospheric fronts rub, and the first ones to detect it are animals. However, some very sensitive people notice the formation of negative ions through discomfort and bone pain, scarring, or headache. It should also be borne in mind that pollution positively ionizes the air so that in large cities and industrial areas, the air, in addition to being of lower quality, will be positively ionized and can cause health problems. Another factor to take into account is the incorporation of chemistry in the food industry that introduces positive ions into the body and, as a direct consequence, has the appearance of free radicals.

Negative ionization in the air is generated for different reasons:

- Storms and other meteorological phenomena such as lightning and wind
- Right after it rains as the rainwater carries the electrons out of the storm
- Natural radiation or radioactivity from land in forests and mountains
- Where sea waves break like rocks and groins
- Rivers very full of water and waterfalls.

All these natural causes generate negative ionization, and we must go outside the house and breathe consciously to take advantage of benefits such as improved mood and increased physical and mental vitality. We must also be aware of what positive ionization in the air hurts us, but always keeping in mind that everyone lives where they live, and if you live in the city, you should not worry about it. But that if we are aware and leave when we can breathe outside the contaminated areas. The walks and excursions to the mountain or the beach will help us to maintain health.

CHAPTER 18

TRICKS TO IMPROVE YOUR BREATHING

Not correctly taking air can cause many health problems, apart from the feeling of overwhelm that it causes. Knowing these techniques will come in handy.

Breathing is practically the only thing in this life that we do unconsciously (and we also don't have to pay for it). However, sometimes you have breathing problems, which is not surprising with the high pollution of large cities, or because of the multiple allergies that are becoming more frequent, or you can feel how you are short of breath or hyperventilating. Believe it or not, breathing well (like everything) can be learned. Several steps can help you.

Stress, anxiety, the posture you adopt, and many other factors can affect the quality of our breathing. Therefore, write down these points that are sure to help you improve your quality of life. Have you never considered your way of taking air before? It's normal, don't worry, but that can change. Set a goal, for example, to do it for 48 hours.

Think about the times when you are under stress. Does it cost you more? Do you need help from the mouth to do it? Do you do it faster or choppy? Study it well, because surely you can improve your ability, like the one who learns to ride a bike.

Posture is essential

We all have a hard time staying straight, even though we are bipeds. Some of us seem to feel a certain nostalgia for the times when we were still hominids, and in the future, we will develop an ideal hump to pass us the lottery tickets in search of luck. In addition to that, posture is closely related to breathing.

Here's the right way: The diaphragm (that is, the muscle that lies between the chest and abdomen and plays a key role in getting air in and out) should not be constricted. Your back has to be upright and your shoulders back and down. The chin should be slightly raised, and the jaw, shoulders, and neck relaxed.

Heart rate

That that deep breathing is healthy is just a myth. If, in addition to making these laments, you also yawn a lot, it is that your body is wanting to tell you something.

Breathing better helps to eliminate stress, but you have to take many factors into account, such as body posture or if you use your nose

When we are stressed or anxious, our heart rate increases, and breathing deeply leads to getting less oxygen, which can increase anxiety and panic. Taking slow, smooth, controlled breaths will be more effective in calming you down if you're stressed or anxious, take note.

Also, too many sighs or yawns, as we said before, can lead you to hyperventilate. Learning to breathe correctly can help, but you may also need to see your doctor for a checkup.

Use your nose

This step is essential to breathe properly. Unless you're doing a vigorous, herculean exercise, try breathing through your nostrils. This helps filter out pollutants, allergens, and toxins when we inhale, and it also heats and humidifies the air. When we breathe through the mouth, the volume of air increases markedly, which can lead to that habit of excessive breathing and increase anxiety.

As a colophon: it also dries the mouth, and we can acquire dental problems. Needless to say, more.

If you start breathing well, this will help you:

- Stop snoring. Surely it is the dream of your partner, who asks every time he has to blow out the candles for his birthday. Snoring can be associated with excessive inhalation due to increased air volume and vibrations. It can lead to non-restful sleep, fatigue, waking up with a dry mouth, sore throat, or headache. Solution? Sleep on your side and avoid eating a lot of drinking alcohol just before bed.
- Eliminate stress. We have already seen that breathing is closely related to nervousness. Restful sleep and being lively and calm will help you breathe well, but when do you notice stress knocking on your door? Take some time to distract yourself, go for a walk. Synchronize the rhythm of your steps with that of your

breathing, so as not to do it irregularly. Having anxiety makes us breathe fast, but breathing incorrectly increases our chances of suffering anxiety, so stop for a moment, think about your diaphragm, calm down and, now, breathe.

CHAPTER 19

MINDFULNESS FOLLOWING THE BREATH

The practice of mindfulness is increasingly expanded in the world thanks to its important benefits. As someone who cleanses his body through a shower, it is important to cleanse our minds by practicing meditation daily, with the help of breathing and preparing ourselves for a better life.

What is mindfulness?

In a world like today, which lives so fast, we are not aware of how we work. We put on autopilot and go outside, we go to work, we eat, we watch TV, and we do a thousand things at once. Mindfulness is being aware of what we do, how our body works. We are aware of all our senses, what we eat, what we feel. Here and now.

Mindfulness is some of the names for this practice that will allow you to increase your quality of life and experience the sensations to the maximum without judging them, just being aware of what is happening at this precise moment.

Through meditation, we get to be in the world in a different way, as we already were when we were children, where our state of full attention was in us as an innate capacity of the human being. Do not confuse meditating with escaping; meditating means being able to be in the present moment as the only real moment.

What role does breathing play?

Breathing is always in our lives, although we hardly pay attention to it. We use phrases hinting at its importance, we say that "we are out of breath" or that we need "room to breathe," but we rarely stop to observe it.

Since childhood, breathing has been our source of energy, and, for this reason, recovering it in this way gives us freedom. To breathe freely, we must not control or judge things, so breathing is presented as a metaphor for our very existence.

The breathing helps us against stress and pain. Observing it will make us realize what happens if we inhabit it and will give us the necessary powers to modify it for our benefit. Meditation and breathing are concepts that go together.

How do you start to meditate?

If you want to learn to meditate, the first thing you should know is that it is not a magic formula. We must practice it to find its benefits. The first thing you should do is find a comfortable place. Some may like a cushion on the floor, a sofa, or a chair at home. Alone or in a group, it doesn't matter, what suits you best, but it should be a quiet place, where you won't be disturbed.

Checking your posture will be the next step. The only really important thing is that you keep your back straight and close your eyes. If you feel sleepy or dizzy when you start, open your eyes a little. We also recommend that you use a blanket since it usually raises the temperature when meditating. Another tip is to put your tongue behind your upper teeth, without applying pressure.

Starting small is important. It may be difficult at first, but long sessions are not necessary; ten minutes is enough to start. Focus on your breathing and your body. And if you can find a meditation group, better than better.

What benefits will meditation bring you?

By practicing meditation, we achieve a series of really interesting benefits that make the art of meditation more and more booming. In general, by meditating, we increase our happiness and our health.

Practicing meditation strengthens our immune system, allowing us to recover before any illness. It also reduces anxiety and insomnia. It favors other points, such as healthy weight loss or increased fertility.

Furthermore, by meditating, we slow down the aging process and increase our emotional resistance, which generally makes us happier.

How do you know if you are meditating correctly?

When we begin to meditate, many of us may think that we will enter a state of absolute peace and relaxation, but this is often very far from reality. The first few times, we may notice tension and itching in parts of the body. If these are the sensations you have when you start to meditate, don't worry, they are normal.

Little by little, you will be able to improve the technique of mindfulness, and you will calm down this inner turmoil and get to enjoy meditation. Keep in mind that the more it costs you, the more you may need it. It is not meditated badly or well, each one has to have his own experience, and all are valid.

Is everything that is said about mindfulness practice true?

The practice of mindfulness has become fashionable, but you have to know how to distinguish what are myths from what is mindfulness in reality. To begin, it indicates that it is not a magic potion. Meditating does not fix everything or solve problems but helps you explore and face them from a new attitude.

You have to know that although meditation is not judging, it is not worth everything. We cannot justify all our irresponsible acts with the "not judging" of meditation. Mindfulness is accepting, but this does not conform, but accepting the situation to seek new solutions.

Also, to achieve the benefits of practicing meditation, you need to practice it daily. Despite what they may say, meditating is not easy; if you are not constant, you will not notice its results, and being constant requires a lot of will.

Dare to start

The practice of mindfulness is recommended for all kinds of people; At first, it requires a little effort and perseverance, but as soon as you see the benefits begin, it will be an essential part of your life.

If you want to start, be patient and prepare to look at life differently, like when we were children. We only cared about the present moment, and that is that when we meditate, we recover that innate capacity, we take off the autopilot, and we embark on attention full. And in this, the Create Health method can help you, which will become your best companion to bring mindfulness and meditation to your day to day. In this method, we also encourage and advise on proper nutrition and more active life.

What differentiates formal and informal mindfulness practice?

The formal practice is the one that we carry out in stillness, sitting, or lying down. We stop for a few minutes, calm the body-mind with the breath, and look inside without judging. We learn to recognize the thoughts and emotions that make up our life experience. We recognize these phenomena as transitory, and we let them pass. We do not expel or remove them. We allow them to disappear, and we surrender to reality: everything is impermanent.

We do informal practice when, in our daily life, we are present: when you eat while eating, say hello, say hello and walk, when you are in what needs to be, living the present instead of filling it with mental noise, constant self-criticism, and anxiety.

One Mindful Day: 17 Exercises In 24 Hours

In the morning

1. You emerge from sleep. Still in bed, make sure for a few seconds to be present, here and now. Before launching into the future of all the tasks that await you, ask yourself kindly how you have slept and how are you. You can also simply "feel" the dawn of a new day, putting all your attention on the physical sensations.

2. Shower with full attention: appreciating the touch of the water, the temperature changes, the smell of the soap.

3. Comb your hair according to the experience on your scalp, the changes in your hair, the movements of your arms.

4. Brush your teeth, putting all your attention on the hand, the brush, the paste, and the sensations on teeth, gums, tongue.

5. Concentrated coffee: or tea, or juice, water. whatever you eat for breakfast. Listen to the sound of the coffee or tea kettle, observe the process of making your drink and awaken your nose with its aroma. Observe the changing colors if you make any mix. Feel the heat of the cup in your hands, the touch on the face of the steam. Finally, analyze the flavor by taking small sips.

6. Any meal or drink throughout the day is used for this exercise of full consciousness. Use food to take a conscious tour of your senses.

7. Move to connect with the Body. Physical exercise is an opportunity for mindfulness practice. Pay special attention to three aspects: breathing, the postures you adopt, and the movements you make, moment by moment. If you are running, listen to the sound of your feet on the ground, feel the air on your skin. If you lift weights, you feel the cold metal bar on your hands. Don't let negative thoughts and distractions take over your body. Let them pass and focus on the body.

At noon

8. Stretch. Take a break at noon and leave the office or wherever you are and do some basic stretching. Wake up like a cat, at ease. In addition to being a very healthy exercise, it is a great opportunity for mindfulness. Look at how your muscles move and appreciate every sensation.

9. Attentive listening: in case you didn't know if you have two ears and one mouth, it is to listen twice what you speak. At least one conversation a day, with anyone you interact with, aim to listen to it with your full attention. When she or he addresses you, breathe, land in the present, and open your sense of hearing. Listen without interrupting, without giving your opinion, without auto-completing the sentences for your interlocutor. This exercise is essential to transform relationships. You will tell me.

10. Do scribble. A conversation between you and me could be this:

-Get a notebook and a pencil, choose a theme and start drawing.

-I don't know drawing. I copied in pre-technology (art education)

-We all can draw. But we have practiced expression much more with words than with images.

-If it is to express myself verbally, I have a university level, I would say. But in the visual expression, I don't go from preschool

-Well, let's leave the word draw aside. Free yourself of responsibility. Pick an idea and start scribbling. Make strokes on a paper concentrating on what is emerging. When you have enough time in front of the screens (they recommend resting every hour) draw a little. Put your full attention there and allow this exercise to be a short break.

Search the visual form of a vague idea helps focus it and leaves bare nonexistent ideas. Sketching requires concentration and trains mindfulness.

11. The self-check. Pause and assess the state of your body and mind. How is your posture? Are you clenching your jaws? Are you thirsty? You will be amazed at what you learn about yourself through these records if you practice regularly. Try introducing these mini checkups more or less every hour. If it works for you, you can set yourself some kind of alarm that alerts you. Ding-dong: connect with your intimacy. Ding dong: keep going.

12. Empty the hard drive. Take 10-15 minutes to sit down with just a pencil and a notebook. During this time, write what goes through your head. Put black on white the thoughts that swirl in your mind. All who arrive, not selected. Like the exercise of putting images to an idea, putting words on it helps clarify it. It is like clearing the forest of the mind. Then it becomes clearer, and you can discover treasures that the undergrowth hid.

At night

13. Out headphones. When you go from home to work or vice versa, avoid the temptation to escape from the environment through helmets. Instead, pay attention to what's going on around you. Listen to the birds sing, watch the children playing in the park, appreciate the different smells along the way. Be fully present.

14. One minute of deep breathing. Focusing on the breath is the quintessential mantra in any meditation school. And it has all the logic. We breathe constantly, but almost always, we breathe unconsciously. Focus a single minute on the breath. Taking that time is a great help in finding the connection to your body. Try this simple, simple breathing exercise: Take a slow, deep breath in through your nose, drawing air in from your abdomen instead of your chest. Pause, holding your breath, before slowly letting the air out through your mouth. As simple as that. Repeat several times and continue with your day of full consciousness!

15. Clean dishes with mindfulness. Getting home and being greeted by a mountain of dirty dishes is no fun. But approaching that task and any other of the house, as an exercise of full conscience, it can be. Feel the water in your hands (or gloves) and study the texture of the sponge as you scrub the dishes with it. This exercise is used to remove dust, hang clothes, make the bed. Don't forget to savor the order and cleanliness when you're done.

16. Musical practice: Music can also be a useful tool to exercise mindfulness in everyday life. Ideally, choose a song you have never heard before and hit play. Do not give thought to the thoughts that arise evaluating the style of the interpreter or the lyrics if you understand it. Let go of all those ideas that appear and listen with your mind and senses open.

17. Try a guided meditation: At this point, we recommend practicing with intimin 10 minutes a day. You just have to follow the itinerary that we have made for you.

CONCLUSION

Breathing is something that is done instinctively throughout our lives, but also instinctively; breathing does not work well in many moments of it.

One of the purest and healthiest breaths is for babies since it is completely natural, complete, and very deep, activating the entire respiratory channel. The abdomen swells and deflates, making us realize the importance of diaphragmatic breathing.

Mistakes we make in breathing

We have made four of the mistakes that we make unconsciously in breathing, but to which we can pay attention to correct them:

- First of all, we don't realize it, but sometimes we don't breathe through our nose. The basis for clean, restorative, clean breathing is that the air must be inhaled through the nose. If we breathe through the mouth, we will be using something that is a resource in normal practice, which should not be the case. The brain, in fact, only reacts to enhance emotional judgments and regain memory when we breathe through the nose.
- Breathing frequency. On many occasions, during stressful moments, we breathe faster. It is precisely in those moments that deep and meditated breathing helps us not lose control. Normally, we breathe, adults, 6 to 8 times per minute. Controlling the frequency of breathing will help us a lot in times of stress but also to better oxygenate the body.
- Where do we breathe from? Most of the time, we are not conscious, but we breathe from the chest when the ideal is to breathe from the diaphragm. We swell the chest when what should swell is the abdomen. It is the best sign to know how we breathe. And of course, if our clavicles are moving when we breathe, we must change it. It is the worst of breaths we can do.
- Finally, the last of the things that we do wrong and that we are not aware of it is that we are not able to dedicate three minutes a day to train our breathing. With this, we will get it to come out unconsciously, naturally, and it will be a great help for our day to day. A few exercises with a portable personal trainer like would help permanently.

Printed in Great Britain
by Amazon

55047287R00061